T0099946

The Three of Us

THE THREE OF US

GROWING UP WITH TAMMY AND GEORGE

GEORGETTE JONES

WITH PATSI BALE COX

ATRIA BOOKS

New York London Toronto Sydney

A Division of Simon & Schuster, Inc.
1230 Avenue of the Americas
New York, NY 10020

First Atria Books hardcover edition May 2011

ATRIA BOOKS and colophon are trademarks of Simon & Schuster, Inc.

Designed by Richard Oriolo

Manufactured in the United States of America

10 9 8 7 6 5 4 3 2 1

Library of Congress Cataloging-in-Publication Data
Jones, Georgette.
The three of us : growing up with Tammy and George / Georgette Jones with Patsi Bale Cox.
p. cm.
1. Wynette, Tammy. 2. Jones, George, 1931– 3. Singers—United States—Biography. 4. Country musicians—United States—Biography. 5. Jones, Georgette, 1970–
I. Cox, Patsi Bale. II. Title.
ML400.J663 2011
782.421642092'2—dc22
[B] 2011000278

ISBN 978-1-4391-9858-2

For my parents,

Tammy Wynette and George Jones

Thanks to you both for your unconditional love, patience, and encouragement, and for sharing your passion for music with me. Thanks for the many life lessons that made me a better person along the way, and for trying to protect me from the world. I pray that you both know how much I love you!

The Three of Us

INTRODUCTION

GO, MOM!

I still remember the day I first saw number 7 in action. I was nine years old, and we were living at First Lady Acres on Franklin Road in Nashville. I had been out on the road with Mom, who'd been playing a long series of shows despite having a broken finger and being in some pain with it. When we got home, my stepfather's teenage nephews, Rodney and Roger, had set up a basketball hoop next to the garage. We were getting off the bus, and Mom heard them shouting, "Hook shot! Hook shot!" One of them dribbled up, went for the shot, and missed.

"That's not a hook shot!" Mom called out.

"What do you know about hook shots?" one of them asked, snickering, as Mom stood there, obviously tired from the trip, her broken pinky finger in a splint held out in front of her.

"I'll show you boys what a hook shot is," she said with a smile. "Throw me the ball, and then you two try to guard me just as if I was a boy. Don't cut me any slack."

The boys were young, strong, and laughing by this time. I was thinking, *Oh, how embarrassing!* Mom was really going to look dumb.

But she caught the ball and started dribbling toward the hoop. She went right around both of them before they knew it, jumped up under the hoop, and sank the shot perfectly.

"Now, *that,* boys, is a hook shot," she said. I started jumping up and down and clapping. Mom winked at me, then sailed on past them and into the house. I was right behind her, and for the first time, I wanted to know all about her high school basketball career. There were many times throughout her life that I was so proud of Mom that I was busting my buttons, but never any more than when she sank that shot.

WHEN I WAS a child, I didn't understand that there was any question about what my mom was *really* like. She was just my mom, certainly not Tammy Wynette: Woman of Mystery. It would be years before I grasped the concept that there were unanswered questions: Was she a symbol of Fragility? Vulnerability? Tragic Southern Gothic? Or was she sturdy little Virginia Pugh, number 7 on Tremont High's 1960 girls' basketball team? I've seen her fragile, vulnerable, and tough. I have seen her sink a perfect hook shot.

I've despaired over the many misguided decisions she made because of the need to have a strong man in her life at all times. And I have felt pride that she was the first single-mother, career-driven singer to brave Nashville broke and alone and become almost an overnight success. I can now understand how those two realities worked together, both for and against her.

People often use the word *tragic* when they talk about Mom's experiences, and while I know she had tragedy in her life, the word shouldn't be glued to her life story. For one thing, human history is full of tragedy, just as it is filled with joy. Mom had both, like everyone else.

As much as people have wondered about Mom, I fear an even bigger mythology has been built on misconceptions about my dad. I think many people believe Dad was some nonstop-partying country music outlaw. He is anything *but* that. In the past, George Jones drank to fit in with the partyers, not because it came naturally. Dad is old-fashioned, shy, and very sensitive. If you get to know him, he loosens up, but it takes a while. In fact, his drinking started after he was out playing in clubs and having to deal with the bar crowd people hovering around, hanging on him. It was almost a defense mechanism, a weapon against his introverted nature. The truth is, he's old-fashioned about almost everything, including how he looks at parenting.

I got a big surprise the first time I had a date on a night that I was staying at Dad's house. I was around fifteen or sixteen. Dad's son, my half brother Bryan, had a brother-in-law named Lonnie who wanted to take me out, and I accepted. I assumed that I didn't need to run it by Dad because he knew the family. So when Lonnie picked me up for a movie, I just left with him. We hadn't made it a half mile when I saw Dad's wife, Nancy, barreling down the road behind us. She pulled up and said we needed to come back to the house before we went anywhere. I must have looked confused, because she started shaking her head.

"I know, I know. But your dad says Lonnie didn't come talk to him. He says he's not letting you go to a movie or anyplace else with someone he hasn't spoken to—no matter who it is. He's never actually met Lonnie, Georgette. The two of you need to have dinner with us."

We went back and ate, and then Dad wanted to spend about thirty more minutes with us. He explained very politely that he just needed to meet Lonnie officially and properly. And *then* we could go to the movies. For Dad, it was the proper way to date.

Dad's much more old school than people may think. And Mom was a lot tougher.

WRITERS HAVE CALLED my parents' marriage a union made in honky-tonk heaven, and to complete that picture, I am told that my birth was hailed as the Birth of Country's Heir Apparent. When I was born in 1970, Billy Sherrill, one of Nashville's most powerful record producers, sent Mom a dozen roses and a signed recording contract for me. The Crown Princess of Country already had a career, all dues paid by her parents.

Whoa! I'm glad that I didn't know about that record contract business when I was a kid. Just standing in their shadows was tough enough. I didn't want any spotlights shone in my direction! It would have been completely out of character for either of my parents to take advantage of that potential opportunity, or to make me feel obligated or entitled to enter the family business. When I finally heard about it as a young teenager, it was almost a throwaway line. Not a big deal. A fun gesture made by the legendary man who produced all those superstars, including Tammy and George.

So many people have asked me about my family so many times. What was it like having these larger-than-life parents? People want to know what a celebrity household is like. Is it wildly different from everyone else's? I guess you'd have to start with looking at how my parents viewed "celebrity," because their attitudes were crucial to our world.

In a nutshell: my mom never trusted stardom, and my dad never liked it.

Except when he is onstage singing, Dad avoids situations where he is a celebrity. For one thing, it surprises him, even after all these years of being considered a legend. He is still a little taken aback when people know who he is or when strangers approach him. He just doesn't get it. I can't even guess how many times he's admitted that he was shocked that people hold him in such esteem. Mom was the same way. She couldn't believe that people from other music genres knew who she was or cared. And if she heard that a movie star or a president was a fan, it never failed to amaze her. In fact, she kept up her beautician's license for many years, *just in case*—just in case it all fell apart.

When I sat down to work on this book, I knew it would be a long and twisted road to discovery. I guessed that one way to look at their complicated relationship was to take a look at how they both came to the marriage—their families, their childhoods, and their paths to country music.

And the place to start is at the beginning.

PART ONE

ROOTS

One

WHEN MY MOM MARRIED MY dad, she was marrying her hero. I'd like to say that right up front, because one speculation I've run across from time to time is that Tammy Wynette wanted to marry George Jones in order to further her career.

Mom's career was doing just fine when she married Dad. She was without a doubt one of the hottest new artists to hit Nashville in a while, with four #1 records and a string of awards and nominations. That's not to say that Mom didn't have insecurities about performing from the very beginning. She even questioned the vocal on her signature record "Stand by Your Man." She did see Dad as the consummate vocal talent. But her career was going strong and in the hands of a man she trusted unreservedly, her producer, Billy Sherrill.

It was her personal life that was shaky, not her career.

Dad was a musical hero to Mom, but it was much more than that. Mom believed she had finally found her Prince Charming. She desperately wanted a champion. Sure, she knew he had a few rough edges when he drank, but like a lot of women have thought about men they loved, she believed she could change him.

She never could change him, but she loved Dad, even as she was leaving him.

Everyone is a product of time and environment, and none more so than Mom. She came along in the rural South just before women started seriously questioning their "place" in the world. She was raised by her grandfather and her stepfather, two good, kind men who respected their wives and loved their families deeply. They were men who would work hard to make sure their wives had what they wanted. Neither of these men had serious torments that complicated family life. My dad was the one who could have told her about having a father with demons to pass along.

Mom was born to Mildred and Hollice Pugh on May 5, 1942, on a six-hundred-acre farm in Itawamba County, Mississippi, just across the state line from Red Bay, Alabama. She called both states home. My grandfather Pugh knew he was dying by the time that Mom, his only child, was born. The brain tumor that was killing him was probably going to blind him first, and he told people he prayed that he would see long enough to have a look at that baby Mildred was carrying. It was an answered prayer. He didn't pass until Mom was nine months old and he had seen his daughter.

Hollice Pugh's death while Mom was just a baby probably had more of an effect on her than she ever knew. But she was lucky in that she had a big extended family and strong father figures to step into her world. Champions.

Mom's mother, Mildred, my beloved MeeMaw, told her that having a child made Hollice's last months of life bearable—holding his baby, sitting at the piano and placing her hands on the keys, talking about his dreams that she would be a musician. He was a multi-instrumentalist, playing guitar, bass, mandolin, accordion, and piano. Mom listened to MeeMaw talk about Hollice's hopes, and they spurred her to learn both guitar and piano. In a way, it's sad that when she made it in music, she put aside the guitar and piano she'd learned. But the truth is, her ability to pick up a guitar and accompany herself helped immensely when she was looking for a recording contract.

The farm where Mom was born was owned by MeeMaw's parents, Chester and Flora Russell. For country people, Chester and Flora were successful and prominent in the county. Still, the Russell household didn't have electricity or a telephone when Mom was little. And whether they are successful or not, farm families usually work in the fields. Mom was no exception as she grew up.

The economic difference between Mom's childhood and Dad's was enormous. Mom did have to do chores on the farm, but it was the *family* farm. There was stability and safety surrounding her. Dad had to quit school at a young age to help out his family. No stability and no safety, just poverty and uncertainty.

In Mom's life as well as mine, the grandparents often took over the parenting role. For Mom, it began when her mother took a job in Memphis to work in a wartime airplane factory. Mom was left on the farm with my great-grandparents, Chester and Flora. Even when MeeMaw returned a couple of years later, Mom always saw her grandparents as parent figures. When MeeMaw moved back from Memphis, Mom moved in with her parents. That caused a little contention from time to time, because MeeMaw was very strict, and Mom knew she could get her way with the grandparents, especially her grandfather Chester. Mom was not above playing her parents and grandparents against one another, either.

Mom dearly loved her steady, rock-solid grandfather Chester, saying, "From him I formed the images I still carry of what a father and husband should be."

When she had her children, Mom ended up like her own mother and was the disciplinarian in the family. I can't speak for Euple Byrd, my sisters' father, but my dad certainly never wanted to be in that role. He couldn't stand the idea of a child being afraid of him, as he had once been afraid of his own father.

When Mom was four years old, MeeMaw married my PeePaw, Foy Lee, and for a time, the two moved into an old, run-down house on the Russell farm. When I say "run-down" I *mean* run-down. Mom said that there were holes in the roof and in the floor, and they literally had to shovel snow out of it in the winter. That's probably why Mom stayed right where she was, with her indulgent grandparents in their nice, big, warm farmhouse. Later, when MeeMaw and PeePaw (Mildred and Foy) moved to

Memphis, Mom went with them. It was short-lived. She was a popular girl who missed both her friends and playing basketball with the school team.

But even though Mom stayed at the home of her grandparents Chester and Flora, she spent a lot of time with Mildred and Foy. PeePaw was a mild-mannered man. I never even heard him raise his voice. Mom said that she saw him lose his temper only one time, when she was about six or seven years old.

PeePaw's father had been a raging alcoholic, far worse than my dad or any of the drinkers I ever knew. After PeePaw and MeeMaw were married, PeePaw continued to help his father take care of his farm, even though he had his own land to work. PeePaw would go over to his father's place after he finished his own chores and get him caught up. It made for long hours, but PeePaw believed it was a son's job to help his parents. He also believed that a husband and father owed his first allegiance to his wife and children. And one of the things he most loved doing was taking MeeMaw and Mom to the county fair. PeePaw, by the way, never thought of Mom as a "stepdaughter," but as his daughter. PeePaw wasn't trying to take Hollice Pugh's place, but he nevertheless considered Mom his child.

He'd been planning on a Saturday at the fair for several weeks, and Mom was revved up about it. He had all the work caught up on both places, so the family set out for the fair. PeePaw decided to stop by his father's house to let him know where they'd be, and that's when the trouble started. PeePaw's dad flew into a drunken rage and started shouting that he needed more help and he needed it right then. He forbade PeePaw from leaving.

Mom said that PeePaw told him very calmly that he would come back the next day, but that he was taking his family to the fair. Then PeePaw's father became horribly insulting, not just toward PeePaw, but toward MeeMaw and Mom, too. PeePaw warned him once. When that didn't stop him, PeePaw knocked him to the ground. Then he got back in the car and took his family to the fair.

"He never explained it or said one word about the incident," Mom said. "I was in complete shock. But the one thing I did understand was that your PeePaw wasn't going to allow anyone to disrespect his wife and daughter. In PeePaw's world, you respected women."

PeePaw also allowed MeeMaw to run the show in most instances. She was the one who was outspoken, the one who laid down the law. PeePaw just wanted to make her happy. I've wondered if Mom might have mistakenly thought all she had to do with my dad was to "lay down the law." That never was a good plan when it came to George Jones. For him, laying down the law was akin to waving a red shirt in front of a bull.

The extended family shaped Mom's circle of friends, too, because she considered her mother's younger sister Carolyn a best friend and sister rather than an aunt. Carolyn was five years older, but the two were very close growing up. They picked cotton and did other farmwork together, played at the family sawmill, washhouse, and barn, and played cowboys and Indians.

Mom was a tomboy who loved athletics more than doll playing, and by the time she made it to high school, she was a killer at the sport she so loved—basketball. Mom was little, but what she lacked in height, she made up for in speed and accuracy. I'd guess I'd always known she'd been a basketball player at one time, but I hadn't ever really thought about it until that day when she showed Richey's nephews her hook shot.

Mom's other early love was music. From the time she was a toddler, MeeMaw had talked to her about her father, Hollice, and his musical talents. Mom knew, for example, that her father had wanted her to have his guitar and to learn to play it well. She heard stories about his holding her at the piano while she was a baby. She took to music naturally, learning to play flute, accordion, guitar, piano, and organ. She had a natural talent, but I also think she wanted to become a skilled musician because it would have made her father proud.

Her feelings for Hollice Pugh took nothing away from her love of her stepfather, Foy Lee. The man I always called PeePaw was a wonderful stepfather. And Mom didn't consider him a stepfather. In fact, the only time I ever saw her lose her temper and cuss someone out was over that very issue. This incident happened in 1988 when PeePaw was dying. Mom was at the hospital, trying to comfort MeeMaw, when a nurse made a remark about Foy "only being" her stepfather. Mom went nuts. She didn't cuss as a rule, but this time the words flew right out of her mouth! She told that nurse in no uncertain terms that she had *no !*%*#! business* describing Foy Lee as "only" anything!

I would never have said anything like that anyway, but as a nurse, I learned that day just how important it is to respect people's relationships.

The hardest thing Mom consciously faced during her early years was having Carolyn nearly die in a car accident.

Carolyn had married and had been in Illinois with her husband for about a year when it happened. It was a head-on collision with a car carrying seven people on their way to a church service. All seven in that car were killed. Carolyn's husband, Gerald, who had been driving, was badly cut. His sister and aunt in the backseat had less severe injuries. But Carolyn hit the front windshield.

She was left with massive injuries, including a horribly scarred face. Her husband was getting ready to leave for the army by the time she was released from the hospital, so Carolyn went home to Mississippi. Mom always said that this experience changed her own life and outlook. She saw how people stared at Carolyn during the time she was going through one painful plastic surgery after another, and she witnessed Carolyn's courage and the way her heart helped her survive it all. I am sure it did make an impact on Mom, because I never knew anyone who cared less about how people looked. If someone had a disfigurement or severe physical disability, Mom saw beauty in him or her anyway. And she had better not hear someone poking fun at those people, either.

That is a character trait my parents shared. Neither of them cared about superficial aspects in others, and they both could be fiercely protective. But when you compare their childhoods, one thing stands out above all else: Mom's was safe, and Dad's was not.

TWO

DAD CAME INTO THIS WORLD George Glenn Jones on September 12, 1931, in Saratoga, Texas, one of eight children born to George Washington Jones and his wife, Clara. It was during the Great Depression, and the Jones family scraped by on next to nothing. The people who got by best were those who could build, repair, haul, and hunt. Dad learned to respect anyone—especially his father—who had what he called "the touch": people who were good at whatever they tried, whether it was repairing a motor or building a log cabin. It didn't take Dad long to figure out how he could best survive: making music.

He was raised in the thickly forested area known as the Big Thicket, a region ripe with musical influences ranging from stone honky-tonk country guitars to Cajun accordions. People who knew Dad as a child said he was very shy for the first several years of his life. It seemed that he emerged from his shell only after he started playing a guitar. But the truth is, Dad never did emerge from that shell. He is still very shy, uncomfortable at parties and events where there are new faces and small talk.

Dad grew up with a father who had a split personality. He was basically a good man—until he drank. Then all the family could do was to try to stay out of his way. George Washington Jones wasn't a drinker until Dad's sister Ethel died from a sudden fever in 1926. Ethel had been the light of my paternal grandfather's life, the adored and cherished first daughter. I've been told that when she passed, my grandfather took to the bottle and never quite made it out.

Dad never knew Ethel. She died five years before he was born. He was closest to his sister Helen, who tried mightily to keep things calm when George Washington Jones stumbled in drunk. George Washington Jones had many jobs over the years, and from all accounts, when he was employed, he was a hard worker. One of his professions was bootlegging, which meant staying one step ahead of both the law who wanted to arrest him and toughs who wanted to rob him. Life was always unsettled. The family moved here and there, living on edge in fear of George Washington Jones going into a rage. The security Dad felt came from his mother, Clara, and from his sister Helen. It was Helen who tried to keep Dad from speaking out when their father was on a tear, who tried to keep the violence to a minimum.

Despite the drinking and fits of anger, Dad did love his father. When Dad was nine years old, his father bought him his very first guitar, a Gene Autry special that Dad has since said was his most prized possession. Singing and playing soon became a way to make his father happy, proud of his son. It especially made him proud when Dad played for people on the street corners of Beaumont and earned money! The old man quickly learned that if he wanted to have access to young George's earnings, he better be right there on the spot, because Dad was prone to running down and blowing it all at the local arcade. Money has never meant anything to my dad. There was a downside to my grandfather's love of Dad's singing, though. Sadly, Grandpa Jones sometimes jerked Dad awake in the middle of the night and made him sing for him. It must have been a horrific experience, but Dad complied out of fear for himself and his mother.

I believe that underneath everything, my dad has always hated the idea that he might somehow put his own family through the risky times he knew as a child. I think he has fought against it, sometimes winning the battle and at other times, losing. Dad has written and spoken about his battle with the bottle, and Mom certainly addressed it in her autobiography. I didn't grow up with it, though. I didn't witness the drinking bouts both my parents have talked about. They hid those from me just as they hid their legendary battles. I did grow up unsure of my dad's love from time to time, but I was never afraid of him.

Despite the glaring differences in their upbringing, Mom's and Dad's lives did share some similarities. For one thing, they both married young the first time. Mom was seventeen when she married Euple Byrd, the father of my older sisters Gwen, Jackie, and Tina. Dad was also a teenager when he married Dorothy Bonvillion, the mother of my sister Susan. Both of these young marriages happened just because both my parents believed that is what you were supposed to do: *get married.* In Dad's case, the marriage was short-lived. It took Mom a long time to leave Euple Byrd, and in those years, she did learn about living with fear and uncertainty.

Mom's marriage happened because my MeeMaw forgot the first rule of dating and teenage daughters: a forbidden boy will attract a girl like a flame pulls in a moth. Despite the fact that Mom was a popular girl—Miss Tremont High—and could probably have dated anybody, she was pulled to Euple, an older guy who liked to party, who had *been around.* And that was precisely why MeeMaw forbade her to see him. A month before she should have graduated from high school, Mom made an end run around MeeMaw, got PeePaw to sign the permission papers, and off she went to marry Euple.

Mom dreamed of a little farm, a house with a picket fence, a house she'd scrub and clean so that her husband would be proud to bring friends home for a fine home-cooked meal. She dreamed of a once-in-a-lifetime love, a Prince Charming who would sweep her off her feet and carry her to that house with the picket fence.

She wanted a fairy tale but ended up in a soap opera.

Mom later said that her hit song "I Don't Wanna Play House" had deep and coincidental roots: "When I was in the second grade, my girlfriend and I built a playhouse. We made furniture out of straw—couches, chairs, beds. It was a wonderful place—until we invited our little boyfriends over to play. They came bearing big bouquets of wildflowers and leaves. The bouquets turned out to be packed with poison ivy. So I guess you could say that my first experience with playing house was more than a little prophetic."

Because she quit school to marry Euple Byrd, Mom took an equivalency test and was not allowed to graduate with her class. She soon had two babies, my sisters Gwen and Jackie, and a husband who seldom worked. Euple moved the family into an abandoned log cabin with no electricity or indoor plumbing.

There was no picket fence.

Her life with Euple was one of hard times and abuse that left her in the depths of melancholy and wanting a divorce. But before she could break completely free from her disastrous marriage in 1965, her husband had the police arrest her and remand her children to the juvenile authorities. She was taken to a hospital for mental health evaluation and saved only because her own physician happened to be on the three-doctor panel that evaluated her.

Now, you would think that MeeMaw, who never liked Euple in the first place, would have come to Mom's defense. But no, MeeMaw saw marriage as an ironclad contract for life, better or worse. By the time Mom was released from the hospital, Euple and MeeMaw had taken the girls to the Pugh home. It's hard to overestimate the emotional damage that experience did to Mom. She must have been terrified, completely beaten down. When Mom finally got her girls back, she knew that she had to leave and try to carve out a life on her own. Nobody was standing by her.

Still, Mom didn't bad-mouth Euple Byrd. It may seem odd that even though in her autobiography she wrote about the bad times in her marriages—put it out there for everyone to see—she seldom talked in negatives about them in front of her daughters. That goes for her final marriage, to George Richey, as well. Only when she was sick and feeling desperate did she open up to any of us about just how bad things had gotten. She fought for her fairy tale until the end.

Three

BECAUSE DAD WAS SEVENTEEN WHEN he married his first wife, he had to get his mother, Clara, to sign her permission. He was already playing music at the time, so when his new father-in-law insisted Dad go to work for him painting houses, the marriage was doomed. One thing about my dad: people should never tell him what to do, whether it is to paint houses or behave like a choirboy. The couple divorced, and Dad signed up for the Marines so he could afford to honor his financial commitment to Dorothy and their baby, Susan. And it was when he was in the Marines that he began to wonder if he could make a living in music.

Country music played a big role in both Mom's and Dad's early lives; Hank Williams was king in the two households. But Mom soon found another musical hero.

When she heard a George Jones and Melba Montgomery duet on the radio, it occurred to her that she, too, might be able to sing on the radio. After all, she believed she was every bit as good as Melba, so *why not*? That thought stayed on her mind, even though she didn't act on it right away.

She put music on the back burner when she married Euple, but as time went by and they seemed to have no prospects, she started working as a waitress and picked up a few dollars singing in clubs. She went to beauty school. Mom had a drive to be something *more*. If Euple wasn't going to get them out of the poverty pit, then she'd have to do it herself.

Mom's first trip to Music City gave her a fever to sing professionally. It was in 1965 when she accompanied two disc jockeys and their wives to Nashville's disc jockey convention. There in front of the Ryman Auditorium, dressed in an old parka and chilled by the cold November wind, Mom approached a band performing on a flatbed truck. The sign read:

WENO Radio—Anybody Can Sing

To Mom, that was almost as good as being allowed to sing at the Opry. She would be right there in front, backed by Nashville pickers.

She climbed up and sang "Your Cheatin' Heart" to a nearly empty street. It wasn't much of a debut, but Mom always said that she returned home fired up. Country legend Mel Tillis recently talked to me about Mom's performing on the flatbed truck that day in 1965. He said he always believed that this moment gave her the resolve to return.

Mom tried to get on as many stages as possible after that, and after singing a few songs prior to a Porter Wagoner show, Porter asked her to go on a ten-day run with him. As it turned out, this was when he was between Norma Jean and Dolly, so Mom lucked out on the timing. She asked her aunt Earleen to travel with her, and later said she had the time of her life opening those shows. But the result wasn't as good as she'd anticipated. Mom drove along behind the bus, picked up her own expenses, and barely had a dime left over from the fifty dollars a night he paid her. Moreover, she wasn't offered a permanent gig. Years later, she was mortified when Porter indicated that he'd slept with both Dolly and Mom! When she complained to Dolly about the comment, Dolly laughed it off, saying that part of the people wouldn't believe him, and the rest of them would just think the two women had bad taste.

Mom loved women who could spit in the eye of an insult, but it was difficult for her to do the same.

Finally, Mom packed up and started for Nashville in her '59 Chevy. Everything she owned was in and on that car. Cardboard boxes were strapped to the roof, tricycles dangled off the sides. Gwen was five years old, Jackie was three, and Tina was fifteen months. It was 1966.

My dad had long been a star when Mom rolled into town with her three little girls. By the '60s, Dad's vocals were already legendary. I don't believe he ever questioned his vocal prowess like Mom did hers. If there was a big difference in their perceptions, though, it might be that Dad saw his music from a blue-collar standpoint. It was something he did well and could use to make a living. When it came to music, he had "the touch."

There's another difference, too. Dad came up through the Texas music world—honky-tonks, small record labels, the building of careers and confidence. Mom walked straight into Nashville's star machine as a hopeful. By the time Dad got around to Nashville, he was a pro.

Dad had finished his time with the Marines in 1953 and returned to Beaumont, Texas, where he went to work as a deejay at KTRM. It was while he played the local honky-tonk circuit that Jack Starnes and "Pappy" Daily, the owners of Starday Records, took notice of him. The next year he released a single, "No Money in This Deal," which didn't chart nationally but got him noticed in Texas. He also met and married his second wife, Shirley.

In 1955, Dad broke through with his first hit, "Why Baby Why," which established him as a songwriter as well as a formidable artist. Nothing interested Nashville more than singers who could write their own hits, and Music Row started paying attention to the guy from the Big Thicket. Then, in 1956, "Pappy" Daily was put in charge of Mercury Records in Nashville, and he brought Dad with him. He continued to have a string of hits including "Color of the Blues," then had a huge release with "White Lightning." That single stayed at the top of the charts for five weeks. Over the next years, he cut some landmark songs like "The Window Up Above" and "Family Bible."

His first duets were cut with Margie Singleton, followed by the work that made my mom sit up and take notice—the Melba Montgomery hits, including 1963's "We

Must Have Been Out of Our Minds." Then, in 1964, Dad moved to United Artists, where he spent six weeks at the top of the charts with "She Thinks I Still Care." In 1965, when Mom made her first trip to Nashville, Dad was at Musicor Records and one of country's biggest stars.

Mom moved into the Anchor Motel in Nashville, where songwriter Don Chapel, the brother of country singer Martha Carson, worked. Don seemed fairly well connected to the business and interested in helping Mom. Lord knows, she needed some help, because she was turned down by almost everyone in town. Moreover, while she made the fruitless trips around Music Row, she had to take her three small daughters with her. Sometimes she brought them into the company offices, but more often, she left them in the car with Gwen in charge.

Finally, record executive Kelso Herston, at United Artists, liked what he heard. Since he had recently signed Billie Jo Spears and didn't think he could break another female artist, he sent her to Billy Sherrill.

Mom got in to see Billy because the woman at the front desk at his office was gone. "You are my last hope," she confessed. Billy said he felt sorry for her that day. She did seem at her wits' end, undernourished, and a little bedraggled. But the image went well with that tear in her voice, and Billy Sherrill never missed spotting unique talent. Billy told her to find some songs and get back to him.

Mom was so lucky to have crossed paths with Billy Sherrill, one of the top producers in Nashville's history. In addition to being a brilliant studio guy, Billy is a genius songwriter, so for my mother to have the opportunity to write with him in those early years is just mind-boggling.

The two of them forged a great friendship that lasted to the day she died.

Mom did as Billy asked, and looked frantically for a song, finally finding one by Scotty Turner, titled "She Didn't Color Daddy 'Cause He's Gone." But Billy was a step ahead of her. He had found a song called "Apartment Number Nine." It didn't top the charts, but it did convince Nashville that Mom was a contender for stardom. And that song introduced her to George Jones.

Mom was invited to hear Dad cut "Apartment Number Nine" at Studio B in Nashville, not as a single, but as an album cut. The thrill of hearing George Jones was overshadowed, though, by her fear that he would bring the song out as a single, and it would marginalize her own cut.

Before releasing "Apartment Number Nine," Billy decided that Virginia Wynette Pugh wasn't particularly commercial and that Mom needed a stage name. He decided on "Tammy" because of the popularity of Debbie Reynolds's character in the film *Tammy and the Bachelor.* He then utilized Mom's middle name, and so she became Tammy Wynette.

She ended up relying more and more on Don Chapel, and finally, when he proposed, she accepted. I think Mom's marriage to Don was one of convenience. Think about her situation: she moved into the Anchor Motel with no money, no friends, and no prospects. Don helped her out with the room, introduced her to people in town, and gave her an ear when she wanted to talk. Mom was lonely and needed help.

Mom didn't have any money even after she signed with Billy Sherrill and released her first single. She still had to take her children with her almost everywhere. Once, when she appeared on Ralph Emery's show, she mentioned the girls. He asked her where they were, and she admitted that they were sitting in the car, out in the parking lot. Ralph almost had a fit.

"Tammy, you don't need to leave those little girls outside in the car! Anytime you come here, you bring them in, and we'll let them sleep on the couch!"

I'm sure those kinds of situations played the major role in her decision to marry Don. She once told me that she knew all along she didn't love him when they married, but she thought that maybe she would fall in love with him over time.

"I was stupid," she said. "I just didn't want to be alone."

Living together without benefit of marriage was not an option as far as Mom was concerned. She knew that word spread like wildfire when it appeared that a "girl singer" was sleeping around. She'd been propositioned by a Nashville producer who assumed she'd be easy pickings—a divorced woman with three kids. And she was determined that she wouldn't be thought of as somebody trying to sleep her way into the business. And so she married for the second time, and once again, it was because it was the thing to do.

FOUR

ALMOST FROM THE BEGINNING, GEORGE Jones seemed destined to play a role in Tammy Wynette's life and career. She freely admitted that she liked being close to Dad once she'd met him and that she'd been overwhelmed by him. Dad was soon interested in her on a romantic level, but fate would shape the evolution of the relationship.

In 1967, Mom had her first #1 release, a duet with David Houston, "My Elusive Dreams." She was booked by Hubert Long, who also booked Houston and George Jones. All of them went out on tour together, and once, in a dispute over David singing with Mom, Houston's manager, Tillman Franks, insulted Mom by insinuating that all female artists slept their way to the top. Mom was furious. And when Dad heard the story via the tour grapevine, he was fit to be tied and stepped in to be her duet partner on the song.

A hero.

About this time, Billy Sherrill found what he believed at the time would be Mom's signature song, her career hit. "D-I-V-O-R-C-E" was written by a man who was on his way to becoming one of Nashville's most important songwriters: Bobby Braddock. He would later pen a song that would play a role in Dad's career: "He Stopped Loving Her Today." Interestingly, both songs needed minor changes before they were recorded. In the case of "D-I-V-O-R-C-E," it was a bit of a melodic change. After that was done, Billy saw it as having huge potential for Mom. And "He Stopped Loving Her Today" required the addition of a spoken part before Dad recorded it.

By then Mom was already having problems in her marriage. Despite Mom's hit records, Don seemed to see himself as the star in the family. He thought it should be his name out front, even to the point of painting "The Don Chapel and Tammy Wynette Show" on the side of the tour bus, as if she were an afterthought. Still, Mom bought them a big home on Old Hickory Lake, three houses down from Johnny Cash's place. The new surroundings didn't make the couple any happier. Meanwhile, Dad got divorced from his wife, Shirley.

Mom learned about Dad's divorce in the spring of 1968, when he stopped by the house to listen to some songs that Don wanted to pitch him. "D-I-V-O-R-C-E" was just out and on its way to becoming Mom's fourth #1. Dad sat down and started singing it. Then he sang it again. And again.

"Did you hear what I said?" Dad asked. Mom thought he wanted to hear how she liked his rendition of her hit. But he quickly corrected her. He was letting her in on a major life change. And I believe that he was letting her know that he was available if she ever decided to get a D-I-V-O-R-C-E herself.

The feelings Mom may or may not have had for Don ended when she learned that he was showing nude photos of her to friends and fans alike. According to Mom, he'd been snapping photos when she stepped out of the shower, when she was getting dressed—anytime that she was in a state of undress. Mom found it annoying that he was snapping photos of her in the bath and the bedroom, but he swore that no one would ever see them, and she believed him. Until he started sharing them.

Mom wrote in her autobiography that she found out about her nude photos in a horrible way, when a fan approached her with one of the photos during a show at the Edison Hotel in Toronto. The event was burned into Mom's mind. She remembered every detail of what that man looked like: bald except for just a little gray around the edges, wearing green pants and a green-and-white-striped shirt. Open at the collar. She was humiliated. When she confronted Don, she learned that he'd been swapping photos with other men through some sort of magazine. He didn't think it was any big deal. (I can only imagine what Mom would have to say about the current climate, where so much damage has been done to unsuspecting people through cell phone cameras and the Internet. I do know that she would have been heartbroken at the suicide of Tyler Clemente, the young gay man who was secretly filmed by a roommate.

She felt extremely close to and protective of her gay friends and fans. One of her favorite honors was having "Stand by Your Man" become a gay anthem.)

Over the next months, as Mom's marriage to Don continued to dissolve, Dad started hanging around. He helped Mom out on a benefit in her hometown, Red Bay, and even had her travel with him when they all played shows together. It had to be obvious that there was a serious mutual attraction. He sometimes visited—often after he agreed to listen to Don's songs. It was when he showed up one night at their house, and heard Don berate Mom and my sisters, that he tipped over the table, told Mom he loved her, and whisked them out the door.

It's no surprise to me that Dad made his declaration of love at a time when my sisters had been insulted. For Don to have insulted Mom was bad enough, but Dad—no doubt remembering his own childhood—could not stand to see or hear young children verbally or physically attacked. That would have pushed him over the edge, drunk or sober. He hates to see women and children bullied. This brings me to another aspect of Dad's personality: he is passionately loyal.

I learned about an incident that speaks to Dad's ferocious loyalty after I started working on *The Three of Us*. It happened in 1983, when Merle Haggard and Leona Williams had just got divorced. Leona had moved back to Nashville and was working hard on songwriting and performing. Dad had been good friends with Merle and Leona when they were married and didn't see why that should change.

One afternoon Leona was being interviewed for a syndicated radio show when the telephone rang. The interviewer told me that as Leona spoke, her voice started to quiver. When she hung up, she explained that her entire fair season was in jeopardy because Merle was threatening a promoter. He didn't want to play shows in venues where they'd booked Leona. This clearly wasn't a friendly divorce!

About this time, the phone rang again. Leona burst into tears as soon as she heard the voice on the other end.

"George, I just don't know what to do! I think Merle's going to keep me off the fair circuit."

She spoke into the phone a few minutes, and then hung up and turned to the interviewer.

"George Jones is such a good friend." Then she shook her head. "I shouldn't have told him about this. He was on his way to a meeting at his label, and now he says he's too upset to go."

To be a third party in that interchange was surprising enough for a new radio reporter, but what happened next was a real shocker. About five minutes later, the door to Leona's Music Row office flew open, and Dad barged in. He demanded to hear the whole story, beginning to end. When Leona finished, Dad grabbed the telephone and called the promoter.

"How could you threaten Leona's tour?" he demanded to know.

The promoter explained that he wasn't doing the threatening. But if he had to choose between booking Leona and losing Merle for the entire season, he'd have to go with the Hag.

"What does Merle think he's doing, anyway? This

just ain't right! And I'll tell you another thing. If you take Leona off the shows, you can take George Jones off, too!" Dad was stone-cold sober. This wasn't liquor talking.

At that point, the interviewer considered turning on the tape, then decided it would be unethical. Perhaps more important, what Nashville newcomer in their right mind would want to get involved in a big mess between Merle Haggard and George Jones?

The whole thing was settled. Leona toured quite a bit with Dad that year, and Merle backed off his hard-line position. Dad and Merle never even mentioned it later when they ran into each other.

It takes that kind of a situation—a friend or family member in trouble—for Dad to go off the rails. He does not like confrontation. In business deals, he'd almost rather take a loss than get into a squabble.

But if someone he liked was in trouble or in a situation where Dad perceived them as powerless, then squabble he would. And it was a result of having seen someone he cared for—and her young children—treated badly that caused Dad to make a stand that night at Mom's home.

After Dad confronted Don, he checked Mom and the girls into a hotel. That proved to be a good move, because Don called the law on them. Officers showed up at Dad's house looking for Mom, but Dad could honestly tell them that she was not there. He didn't mention that he had them stashed at the Hilton.

A couple of days later, Mom and Dad flew to Mexico City, where Mom filed for a divorce from Don. But as it turned out, Tennessee didn't recognize Mexican divorces, and Don filed a lawsuit against Mom and Dad: desertion, adultery, alienation of affection. But in a strange twist of fate, it turned out that Mom hadn't been divorced from Euple Byrd for one year (as Alabama law required) when she'd married Don in the first place. The marriage to Don was annulled.

Hoping to avoid being the object of more gossip, Mom and Dad announced that they got married in August of 1968, just before they moved into Mom's house on Old Hickory Lake. That presented a bit of a problem. Because people already thought them married, they had to be careful about when and where they really did tie the knot! And so they were finally wed in Georgia on February 16, 1969. Dad told her she shouldn't show the marriage certificate around because then everyone would know they'd been lying about the first wedding. *Oh, what a tangled web.*

At the time Mom served divorce papers on Don Chapel, she was recording "Stand by Your Man," the song that would become her theme, a defining lyric, and the subject of far too much analysis when it came to Mom's life and attitudes. Mom didn't see it as an anthem of any kind. To her it was just a love song that Billy Sherrill had started and that she had helped him finish. He had originally thought of writing a song called "I'll Stand by You, Please Stand by Me," inspired by the Ben E. King song "Stand by Me." In the end, Mom and Billy sat down toward the end of a session, changed the title to "Stand by Your Man," and finished the song.

Mom didn't like the melody, specifically the high notes. She very seldom questioned Billy Sherrill about any of his decisions, but this time she did, begging him not to release the song as a single. "I sound like a pig squealing on those high parts," she said. To make matters worse, when she played it for Dad, he wasn't impressed. Mom respected his judgment, so his viewpoint only proved to her that she was right. Billy wisely ignored her protests, and Epic Records released "Stand by Your Man" on October 19, 1968. It stayed at #1 for three weeks.

Careerwise, two things happened simultaneously: Mom and Dad started playing more shows together, and Billy Sherrill started talking to Dad about getting out of his Musicor contract and signing with Epic. That was the only way Billy could cut the duets he was chomping at the bit to record. The shows were easier to pull off than the record deal. Once they finished up their immediate contractual obligations, they could be promoted as a double billing.

One song overshadowed the first years of my parents' life together: "Stand by Your Man." The song propelled Mom into superstardom in 1968 and kept getting bigger even through 1975, when it hit #1 in the United Kingdom. She won a Grammy, the Top Female Artist award from the industry magazines *Cashbox* and *Record World*, several top sales awards, and she started a three-year reign as the Country Music Association's Female Vocalist of the Year. Between the career-making release of "Stand by Your Man" in 1968 and the first #1 duet with Dad, 1973's "We're Gonna Hold On," Mom spent over twenty weeks at the top of the country music charts.

Mom was very lucky to have married not just a legend, but one who also paid very little attention to star status. A lesser man might have resented that reign at the top of the charts.

FIVE

MOM SAID THAT DAD TAUGHT her a lot of things during their marriage. As she put it, "I was just a farm girl when I came to Nashville." She believed that Dad was a big help to her in understanding the country music business. He didn't care much for it, but he knew how it worked. Mom said many times that during the years after they divorced, her regard for Dad did nothing but grow. Once she stepped back from their problems as husband and wife, she was able to appreciate him as a person.

She learned one skill from Dad that might surprise some: home design.

Mom started getting her "decorating degree" from the George Jones School of Design during the year they lived together (and pretended to be legally wed) at the Old Hickory house. As she wrote in her autobiography: "I had never known a man to be so interested in decorating, and since I knew nothing about it myself, I was fascinated to watch him at work. He'd surround himself with samples of wallpaper, fabric, and carpeting, and he knew exactly what he wanted for every room."

Mom said that Dad would walk through furniture showrooms, pointing at one item after another for every room in the house, including two rooms that he added to the house. He always knew where things were going, what colors and textures worked together, and what the final room design would look like. Mom said that it was as if he had a blueprint in his mind. He had good taste and knew what he was doing every step of the way.

Mom carried his love of design with her. I'm remembering an incident that happened long after she and Dad were divorced. Mom was living on Franklin Road in Nashville, and planning a small living room that opened onto the kitchen. She decided to bring in a professional. It was decided that the room would be done in cream and black: stark, classy, distinguished. One evening after the decorator left, Mom sat looking at the room and studying fabric swatches for a long time. By the next morning, she'd decided to hang deep-watermelon-pink-colored drapes.

"You can't do that!" the decorator insisted. "It will look terrible!"

Mom was firm. She wanted watermelon drapes. And so they were ordered and installed, with the decorator shaking his head every step of the way. But once they were up, he stood back wide-eyed.

"Fabulous! Absolutely perfect!"

She would be the first to tell you that she learned it all from George Jones.

IN MARCH OF '69, a month after the official wedding, Mom and Dad moved to a home Dad owned in Lakeland, Florida. Mom said that part of the reason she wanted to leave Nashville was because of all the gossip that had surrounded her splitting from Don and moving in with Dad. Not only did the tabloids have a field day with the story, but there also had been a huge headline on the front page of the *Nashville Banner* that read: "Tammy Wynette Leaves Husband for George Jones." That kind of publicity may not bother some celebrities, but it mortified Mom.

Once in Florida, Dad immediately started redecorating. But this time he ended up having bigger dreams than sprucing up a living room. Not long after they moved to Lakeland, Dad saw a house he couldn't resist. It was located just outside of town, down a long, winding road through citrus groves. It was an old plantation-style home with sixteen rooms, each one in a worse state of disrepair than the last. Mom couldn't believe Dad had fallen in love with a house needing a complete overhaul. Of course, for Dad, that was part of the attraction. He was itching to remodel from top to bottom. Better yet, the house came with five acres that he could landscape.

Mom hated the whole idea. She hated the ugly paint on the cracked walls (one bedroom was orange and green), the creaking floors, and the out-of-date kitchen appliances and plumbing fixtures. When Dad told her what a great buy it was at $100,000, all she could think was, "It's a money pit!"

So Dad played his ace, the idea that the place could pay for itself because he also planned to build a country music park on the land.

A what!?

A country music park.

It made perfect sense that Dad loved the idea and perfect sense that Mom didn't. For my dad, it meant staying home most of the time. No matter how much he seemed to be the ultimate road dog, running all over the country to one rowdy club after another, Dad wanted to be sitting in his own house, feet propped up, watching a ball game on television. The idea that he could put on country music shows was secondary to the idea of his not having to go anywhere. He could have it all—make his music and be a homebody. He built and opened quite a few clubs and music parks over the years. But the one in Lakeland was probably his most ambitious.

The whole thing scared Mom from a financial standpoint, but there was also a part of her that liked the idea that her husband would be tied to home, easily available for his shows, and hopefully, making money from it. Of course, Dad was always coming up with business ideas. One of the first things he did after they moved to Florida was to invest in a trailer park, which he called Tammy's Courts. He even dug the sewer lines himself.

Dad was really happy during that time. He invested in the trailer park, several rental properties, and other commercial interests. He loved doing business—note that I said "doing" business, not "taking care" of business. Dad is an idea man. He is wonderful when it comes to the idea and initial work that it takes to get something going. He doesn't want to handle details down the road, though, so some accountants and day-to-day caretakers better be on hand. For him, it's all about the creative end of things. And he is brilliant at it.

He threw himself into both the house renovation and the country theme park, which he decided to call Old Plantation Music Park. He spent hundreds of thousands of dollars on his park, traveling all over the South picking out the right trees and shrubs, putting in fish ponds, and, of course, building his stage. Dad cleared the brush on the acreage himself. He does love anything connected to yard work! The trouble was, according to Mom, he got so far into the whole thing that he didn't want to go out on the road to play shows, which was how they were financing the whole operation.

Mom loved cooking for Dad. She started making him her famous ham and dumplings, chicken and dumplings, biscuits, banana pudding. Dad admitted to gaining forty pounds within a year of their marriage because of Mom's cooking. Having gone from a 29-inch waist to a 34, he ended up giving sixteen too-tight, never-worn suits to Johnny Rodriguez.

Mom was pregnant with me while all this was going on. Luckily, they had a lot of friends and family around them. Dad's road manager, Billy Wilhite, moved to Lakeland, and in addition to taking care of Dad's career, he managed Tammy's Courts. Mom and Dad bought her parents a nice house in Lakeland. Mom's father's parents were elderly, and so they came to live at the court as well. Mama Pugh and Dad got to be really close in those years, and they stayed friends even after my parents were divorced.

Because drinking always comes up when anyone mentions George Jones, I want to go on record to say that he wasn't the only one imbibing back in those days. Certainly half of Nashville was swigging whiskey. There were other legendary drinkers from Tex Ritter to Ernest Tubb. And that's just liquor. Then we'd have to start talking about popping pills. And there was some drinking going on around the Jones household that involved more people than my father.

Mom told this story about our family, liquor, and the local dog track. One time when Dad's mom, Clara Jones, was visiting, Mom and Dad took her and Mama Pugh to see the dog races. My grandmother Jones, in particular, was mortified because she was a Pentecostal and she feared if word got back to Texas she'd be kicked out of the church. When Mama Pugh wanted something to drink, Dad ordered her a screwdriver. She took a few sips.

"George, I feel a little light-headed."

"Well, Mama Pugh, maybe you'd better not drink any more of it," Dad quickly said.

"Why, what do you mean? I *like* it. It's right refreshing!" And Mom said she finished the drink.

But there's another dog track story. It involves my grandfather PeePaw.

PeePaw went to the track with some friends of Mom's, and they started ordering drinks all around. PeePaw obliged and had some cocktails that hit him like a brick on the head. Mom's friends decided to take him back to the car while he could still walk. They hauled him to the parking lot and got him propped up in the backseat. Then they started worrying that PeePaw might rouse himself and wander off. They talked it over and figured out that if he had no shoes, he wouldn't start walking around. So they removed his loafers and left him there.

When they returned, PeePaw was nowhere to be found. They were still driving around looking for him when Mom got a call from the police.

"We have your dad down here at the police station," the officer said. "Who is this?"

It turned out that PeePaw had refused to identify himself. The police finally convinced him to call a friend or relative, and as soon as he dialed, they took the phone from his hand. It turned out that they had found him walking around drunk in his stocking feet and arrested him. They nearly died when Mom identified herself.

"Oh, Miss Wynette, if we'd known who he was, we wouldn't have arrested him. He wasn't hurting anything. But we worried he was going to get hit by a motorist. He's free to go, but somebody will have to drive him home."

Mom ran through the house, gathered up some photos and record albums, jumped in her car, and gunned it to the police station. She signed the memorabilia and apologized to the officers. In the end, they tore up the arrest report and sent him on his way. PeePaw was mortified. He told Mom that when he finally realized that he'd been arrested, he was afraid to tell them who he was for fear of embarrassing her.

"I thought I'd just stay in jail until somebody came looking for me," he said.

PeePaw got off easy that time. Mom had more tolerance for his drinking than she did for Dad's.

One time when Dad was missing in action, Mom asked

PeePaw to go look for him. She told PeePaw he needed to look in every bar, every hangout, and every friend's house until he found Dad.

"Then you drag him home!" Mom instructed.

Several hours later, PeePaw showed back up and literally fell out the door of the car, dead drunk. He pulled himself off the ground and staggered up to the house, where Mom stood staring at him, her jaw dropped in surprise.

"Don't tell Mildred," he said. But it was too late. MeeMaw was standing right behind Mom, as furious as Mom was shocked.

"Well, where is George?" she asked, her voice stony.

"Well, when I was getting ready to leave that last bar, George was getting ready to head to another one," PeePaw answered.

"It was *your* job to bring George home, Foy Lee!" MeeMaw was clearly not amused. "Why in the world would you start drinking with him?"

"Well, I tried to convince him," PeePaw explained. "But then George bought me a drink. And every time I said, 'Let's go home,' he bought me *another* drink. I didn't want to bother anybody, so I drank 'em."

MeeMaw was *hot*!

"Well, you are not sleeping in this house in this condition," she said. "I won't have it! You can just go sleep in the barn."

PeePaw was wandering off in the direction of the barn when he spied the motor home parked off to one side.

"Hell, I decided I'd just go sleep in that RV," he later said. "It had a pretty good bed."

Now, remember—my MeeMaw could be tough. Back

when Mom married Euple Byrd, MeeMaw was the one who decided that my mom had made her bed and she should have to sleep in it. She even helped Euple hide my sisters from Mom. So as wonderful as she was to us grandkids, she could be rough when it came to adults. And when she saw PeePaw go inside that RV, she really got fired up. The idea of his sleeping on a nice comfortable bed instead of in the barn was more than she could stand. So she grabbed the garden hose, marched over, and started shooting a steady stream right in the window of the RV's bedroom!

PeePaw finally staggered back outside, not only on the verge of passing out, but also sopping wet.

"Oh no you don't," she said, fuming. "You will not go in there and have a nice night. That's why you don't get to sleep in the house. You go sleep in the barn like I told you to do!"

PeePaw slunk off and slept in the barn.

These days they'd probably have been offered a reality show.

PART TWO

HOT A'MIGHTY!

Six

I ALWAYS LOVED LISTENING TO Mom talk about the night I was born. She said that when she was giving birth, Dad got so excited out in the fathers' waiting room that he jumped in the air, clicked his heels together, and shouted, "Hot a'mighty!"

It was October 5, 1970.

They'd been trying to get pregnant for months when one night after a show in Atlanta, Georgia, Dad lit a cigarette and it made Mom queasy. Dad was a little surprised because they both were smokers. Mom had been smoking cigarettes since she was a teenager. Then it hit Mom. There was *one* thing that made her sick around smoke: being pregnant.

The two of them were so anxious to find out if a baby

was in their future that they went to a doctor in Lakeland to be tested as soon as they got home. They didn't even make an appointment—just showed up. The minute they got back to the house with the positive result, Dad was on the phone to Texas, calling friends and relatives, sharing the good news.

It was big news around Nashville and among their fans worldwide. The marriage had been considered the stuff of legends, and having a baby made it picture-perfect. There was another side to the story. Few fans at that time knew that behind the scenes there were beginnings of discord related to drinking and control issues. Mom was busy trying to change a man who was digging in his heels. Although real trouble stayed on the back burner, between working on a theme park and waiting on a baby, it sat there simmering.

Mom worked out on the road up until the week before I was born. She thought it was hilarious that when she awakened Dad a little after midnight to tell him she was in labor, he started looking for his avocado green pants and green-and-white-striped shirt. (I guess it's his design gene.) Dad likes to be color coordinated. But that wasn't the thing that most surprised Mom that night. What shocked her was his overall demeanor. Dad was completely composed. There was no speeding through the streets, no panic. It was almost as if he was trying to make sure *she* stayed calm. He didn't freak out even once during the drive, and in fact, calmly talked to her about how the orange crop in Florida was doing.

The minute they wheeled Mom into the delivery room, Dad let out his "Hot a'mighty" holler and immediately got back on the phone to Texas to let his family know the baby was coming. He has since said that when told his daughter had arrived, it was one of the highlights of his life. Mom wasn't quite so excited. She thought that Dad wanted a boy, and it took some convincing for him to make her understand that the baby they'd had was the baby that he'd wanted: healthy, with ten toes and ten fingers. A little girl? That was wonderful.

Here's how Mom described his reaction in her autobiography:

"I vaguely remember being wheeled to my room after the delivery. George told me later that I kept apologizing to him for having a girl. He leaned over the bed and kissed me and said, 'Oh, honey, you don't know how happy you've made me. I wanted a girl all along because I wasn't around when Susan was a baby, but I thought *you* didn't want a girl because you already had three! That's why I said I wanted a boy. Wait until you see our daughter. She's the prettiest little thing in the whole nursery.' "

I could have quoted those words long before I ever picked up a copy of *Stand by Your Man*. She'd told them to me often enough.

Mom said I looked just like Dad, a miniature George Jones. She especially saw him in my eyes. When she told him that, he scoffed at the idea. "Oh, I didn't notice that. I don't think she looks like me."

Then he ran back to the telephone to call everyone back to say that the baby looked just like him. According to Mom, that's when Dad started to fall apart. He started drinking one cup of coffee after another and got so wound up the doctors thought they might have to sedate *him*.

When they brought me home, Mom and I were greeted with a plaque engraved with three love poems Dad had written about his wife and little girl. Mom said that she nearly fell apart, seeing this openly tender, romantic side of the usually *very* private George Jones.

It brings tears to my eyes to think about Dad's reaction to my entry into their world: *Hot a'mighty!*

I WAS A daddy's girl from the beginning, probably because he was the one who insisted that I sleep in their room instead of in the nursery attached to the master bedroom. Mom said I was soon spoiled and knew that all I had to do was cry and Dad jumped. Tina was said to have been a little jealous, because she had previously held the coveted "baby of the family" position. But Dad quickly convinced her that he had enough "father" in him to go around.

Dad loved Mom's girls and considered them his own. In fact, when Tina came home from school in tears, saying that the teacher wouldn't let her use the name Tina Jones, Dad adopted all three. Although he later was a part of my sisters' lives, Euple Byrd didn't protest the action at the time. I know that part of Dad's mind-set was that he wanted a second chance at being a parent, feeling that he had fallen short the first time around.

Likewise, my sisters adored George Jones. He spoiled them just as he later did me. Jackie has said that all they had to do was mention some toy or game, and he'd come home with it. There was never a question with Dad as to what he'd married—he'd married a woman with three daughters, a family. The three had very different personalities, too.

Of all my sisters, Tina is the most like Mom, and that could be both funny and upsetting to watch play out. Tina is decisive, strong-minded, and willful at times. Don't tell her she can't do something, because she will be determined to do it. Likewise, don't say "you *have* to" do this or that. She does not take well to a show of authority. Mom didn't like it when her mother bossed her, and Tina didn't like it when Mom did. But like Mom, Tina has a kind and caring side.

On thinking about it, my three older sisters fit the typical child-order personality profiles, with Tina being youngest and least afraid of confrontation. Jackie, the middle daughter, hated controversy and confrontation, trying to be politically correct at all times. That's why I was shocked when Jackie decided to write a book about Mom's death, detailing all the problems with our stepfather, George Richey. She was the last person I'd have expected to speak out. I'm probably more like Jackie than I am my other two sisters. I don't like controversy, either.

Like so many other firstborn children, Gwen was always a more parental figure. Gwen was ten years old when I was born, and from what I am told, she carried me around a lot of the time. She was and is a take-charge, hardworking person, an organized list maker. She does share Mom's and Tina's stubborn gene. I'm sure she felt enormous pressure when Mom first moved to Nashville, because even though she was still a small child, she was often in charge of Jackie and Tina.

That's the family into which I was born: two country singers who were trying to build a country music theme park near Lakeland, Florida; three sisters with very different personalities; grandparents; great-grandparents—all living within walking distance of one another. Of course, the extended "family" also included an assortment of friends, roadies, personal assistants, managers, and musicians.

My earliest and most vivid memories are of riding on my dad's lap while he mowed grass at the Florida property. I must have been around two years old. It still brings up memories of feeling safe, of being loved—and smelling newly cut grass, something I love to this day.

From what I have heard, Dad was sober much of the time while he was working on his music park, the more serious drinking started up again when the venue was operational. Dad was on a natural high during the planning stages. For one thing, he was able to showcase his pride and joy: the car collection. What an amazing assortment of classic vehicles it was, too. Among his most prized were a 1940 Lincoln Zephyr, a 1923 Cadillac, a 1936 Chevrolet, a German Steyr, and a 1929 Model A Ford. In his autobiography, Dad described one of the most unusual:

"I bought a Pontiac that Nudie [the clothing designer] had converted. It was a white convertible, and there was a plastic dome to shield the interior. The dome was in the shape of a bubble like those used by presidents seeking protection from assassins. (Mine wasn't bulletproof.) Nudie embedded four thousand silver dollars in the dashboard, console, doors, and a part of the floor. The console was actually a saddle."

The greatest thing about that car was that Dad had a tape of a cattle stampede he could play while he drove around in it.

Dad's car collection is one of the reasons Mom always accused him of being a little boy who never grew up, who just got more expensive toys. But she went right along with it, too. Once when he was looking at antique cars, Dad spotted a Model T Ford with a rumble seat that he fell in love with. Mom talked him into waiting to buy it, then went behind his back and bought it for him. He had a fit when he learned someone else had purchased it—until Mom had it delivered. They loved buying things for each other.

On opening day, Old Plantation Music Park had everything from peacocks and flamingos to carnival rides and hot dog stands. Anyone buying a ticket to the music show got to see the cars free of charge. There was an expensive, state-of-the-art sound system, top-quality dressing rooms for the artists, and a roof over the bleachers to protect fans from too much sun or the occasional rain.

Dad has said that he was nervous about filling the park that day, especially given that he'd spent so much time and money on the place. Also, in a way, his reputation was on the line because he'd booked some big country artists. Conway Twitty was the headline act, with Charley Pride the special guest star. The press was covering the opening on the ground and from the air. Helicopters hovered over the park with cameramen leaning out the sides. And all the hard work paid off. They sold out the park and had to turn ten thousand people away!

Billy Sherrill came to Lakeland for the grand opening. He had good reason to want to see what was happening, because he was planning on adding George Jones to the Epic Records roster. That seemed the only way Mom and

Dad could record the duets that Billy believed they could turn into country gold. Dad just had to get out of his deal with Musicor. For Dad's part, he saw it as both a tempting opportunity and a lingering concern. There was no doubt that Billy and Epic had national and even international clout. Moreover, Billy's reputation was beyond question. He was as good as it got when it came to making hit records. Dad wanted assurances that the Nashville Sound Billy represented wasn't going to dilute the stone country music that was George Jones's trademark.

The real eye-opener might have been just getting Billy Sherrill out of Nashville to attend a big out-of-doors show. He wasn't known for heading off on junkets. But for Mom and Dad and the Plantation Park, he made the trip. A lot of Nashville and country music's best did, as well.

So many of my parents' friends played the park during its run: Merle Haggard, Waylon Jennings, Johnny Cash. Loretta Lynn headlined. The Statler Brothers. Tom T. Hall. The Carter Family. Thinking about the Carter Family reminds me of an attitude I believe Dad shared with Mother Maybelle. I've read that Mother Maybelle saw her music career as a regular job, something she did to earn a living. She didn't see that it set her apart from anybody else or elevated her. It was simply what she did. That sums up how Dad sees it, too.

Mom usually invited everyone up to the house for meals while they were in town. Nothing made her happier than cooking for a crowd. And while she appreciated praise for her singing, she *loved* people who complimented her down-home food! The hands-down favorite among the guests was always her banana pudding.

From everything I have heard, my parents were the happiest when they stayed at home and put on shows at the Old Plantation Music Park. Ralph Emery once told Mom and Dad: "Yours is one of the happiest homes I've ever been in. Good food. Good friends. Good feeling."

Ralph says that during those early days, Mom babied Dad half to death. When she suggested Dad let his short haircut grow, he protested that he wouldn't be able to keep up any other sort of hairdo.

"Jones, with those big ears, and that buzz cut, you look like a cab coming down the street with both doors open," Mom laughed.

"I guess I just hired me a hairdresser," Dad answered.

Mom began blowing his hair dry every morning. "George can honestly say he carries that hairdresser he hired with him everywhere," she said.

Dad responded: "I married the best hairdresser, the best cook, and the best singer in the world. But more important than that, I married the best person in the whole world."

SEVEN

THE FLORIDA PARK WAS NEITHER the first nor the last of Dad's ventures into country music venues. He owned clubs in Texas and Tennessee both before and after he was married to Mom. In one way, his love of owning clubs and outdoor music sites isn't surprising. In the rough world of Texas honky-tonks, where he honed his art, club owners or fair and festival promoters held a lot of power. If they wanted you to sing cover songs—other people's hits—instead of your original material, that's what you sang. And if they wanted the singers to mingle and party with the clientele, then mingle and party was the name of the game. For the record, Dad's park in Florida was strictly nonalcoholic, a teetotaling, family-friendly experience.

It did well in those early years. In fact, the park made

enough money to finance a succession of grand vacations where Mom and Dad played host to both family and friends. They went to Hawaii, Mexico, and the Bahamas. Those were their golden years, when their marital difficulties seemed like they could be handled.

Once the Old Plantation Park was open, the George and Tammy duet plan took precedence. Dad bought his way out of the Musicor contract, although it cost him dearly. Once he made the decision, he was willing to pay the price to make his move.

Both careers, Mom's and Dad's, were perfectly positioned with big solo hits to help turn a series of duets and the resulting tours into something for the history books.

Dad had some big songs in his last years on Musicor: "Walk Through This World with Me" in 1967, "I'll Share My World with You" in 1969, and "A Good Year for the Roses" in 1970. Once on Epic, he had more high-impact releases, including "A Picture of Me (Without You)" and two #1 songs—"The Grand Tour" and "The Door"—in 1972.

Mom had chart-topping releases following "Stand by Your Man," as well. But even though "Singing My Song" and "The Ways to Love a Man" each stayed at #1 for two weeks in 1969, and "He Loves Me All the Way" also hit the top in 1969, they couldn't quite get out from under the shadow of "Stand by Your Man."

Nor could the first of the duets compete with Mom's and Dad's solo releases at the time. They started recording duets in 1971. Those songs became country classics, cementing the two together forever no matter what their marital status. But beginning with 1971's "Take Me" through 1973's "Let's Build a World Together," the first four duets didn't set the music charts on fire.

The duet that hit #1 and stayed there for two weeks was 1972's "We're Gonna Hold On," which was appropriate given their sometimes on-the-rocks marriage status. Following that release, the two recorded a fan favorite even though it made it to only #15 on the charts: "We're Not the Jet Set."

They were, of course, something of a jet-setting couple. They were burning through their cash like crazy. Keeping up with the Joneses in the early 1970s would have been a tough proposition because they were a one-couple economic stimulus. Dad loved cars, and Mom bought them for him. Mom loved furs and jewelry, and Dad bought them for her. Maybe they thought new things would take their minds off the problems that were starting to grow more prominent as time and tours went by.

Mom and Dad playing shows together on the road turned out to be good promotion for their recordings, professionally strategic, but personally contentious. Dad wasn't used to having a caretaker. He was always tough to figure out when it came to playing shows. For example, most stars want to make sure they close the show as a matter of respect. But Dad didn't care who closed. He would rather open the show so he could go back to his hotel room and watch television.

If pressed about his drinking, Dad dropped out of sight, which drove Mom crazy. An aside: some have thought that Dad's habit of disappearing might have been why he was nicknamed "Possum." In reality, that name was given him by deejay T. Tommy Cutrer, who thought that on one of Dad's album covers, his hair looked like Pogo in the comics.

Mom couldn't believe that Dad wouldn't listen to her, and she reacted as one might expect, by staying after him about his habit. After all, MeeMaw had been able to shut down PeePaw's interest in liquor with a couple of wifely smackdowns. That didn't work with Dad. Mom tried the same technique of husband control, and it is where their famous line came from, the one explaining how the two of them might have stayed married. Once, when appearing on Ralph Emery's television show, they agreed that it would only work if Dad quit nippin' and Mom quit naggin'.

Dad often shook his head over the fact that Mom tried to change him. She knew he liked to drink when she married him, and it irritated him that she seemed surprised when he did just that. Another thing that annoys him is the idea that he had completely gone off alcohol during the early years of the marriage, then suddenly, for some inexplicable reason, jumped back in a bottle and went 'round the bend. He says he never completely quit to begin with, that he had continued to drink through the whole marriage. He just cut down from time to time.

That reminds me of a funny story songwriter Larry Lee used to tell about Dad and bad habits. Larry Lee wrote for Cedarwood Publishing, the once powerful company founded by Opry manager Jim Denny and superstar Webb Pierce. Word around Nashville during the early 1980s was that Dad was completely sober, that he hadn't touched a drop of alcohol in months. Dad stopped by Cedarwood to talk songs with his friend Larry one afternoon. Dad was smoking a cigarette when he opened the door.

"George! Good to see you!" Larry said. "You know those are gonna kill you," he added, motioning toward the cigarette.

"Well, Larry, somethin's got to," Dad quipped.

"Is it true that you quit drinkin'?" Larry asked.

"Sure is."

"Really," Larry answered in a suspicious tone of voice.

Dad nodded. *Yes, really.*

"Completely?" Larry still didn't buy it, even though Dad stood there sober as the proverbial judge.

"Well, not completely," Dad said. "I still sip along on Amaretto most days. But I ain't *drinkin'*."

THE EVENTS THAT happened in Florida in 1971 and '72 are classic "he said/she said."

Mom wrote in her autobiography that Dad got drunk and started shooting off a gun.

She said he tore up the house.

Dad says he doesn't believe he did either thing.

He said/she said.

In a move that somewhat mirrored what had happened to Mom years earlier, she had Dad hauled away and evaluated by doctors. Dad says he was so alone that he had to take a cab home after spending ten days in a padded room. He arrived back in Lakeland feeling sick, sad, and sorry. To top it all off, he walked into the house to face a mess he swears he didn't make. Mom was on the road doing some Canada shows, so Dad went to work and cleaned up the house. Then when Mom got home, they didn't talk about it.

Mom said that when she was out on the road, Dad used to ask her grandma Pugh to come play gospel songs on the piano for him. He would confess that he was drinking too much and explain how he loved Mom. Grandma Pugh would tell him to pray and trust that the Lord would answer. But in the end, Mom said he would go out and start drinking. It almost always ended with him heading to Texas or to Nashville, where he could find old drinking buddies.

Once, after Mom insisted Dad see a doctor about his face becoming bloated, he was told that the liquor was scarring his liver and could eventually kill him. The information made him drink even more. His idea was that if he was dying anyway, he might as well have a good time on the way to the cemetery. That attitude infuriated Mom.

One of the worst times happened during the 1971 Disc Jockey Convention in Nashville. Epic Records planned on introducing Dad as their new superstar signing, but Dad was, according to Mom, drunk and belligerent. That should have been no surprise to the CBS executives, because they'd been with him that afternoon, drinking and watching ball games at the hotel. But by showtime, most of the executives were sober, and George Jones was just getting started. Mom arrived alone at the Ryman Auditorium, upset, crying, and her hair in a mess. That's how she met her friend Jan Smith, who was working with Johnny Cash at the time. Jan saved the day by putting Mom's hair and face back together, and the two became lifelong buddies. But Mom never forgave Dad for the embarrassing incident.

Those were days and events I can't address or explain. My sisters remember nothing violent during the time. Whatever it was, it happened away from children's eyes and ears. I do know that when it comes to high-stress life situations such as divorce, we each create our own version of the truth. I suspect it's usually somewhere in between the two stories. Not surprisingly, their troubles did not end with Dad cleaning up the house. He dropped out of sight a few more times before he finally did stop drinking for about a year.

From the time that Dad had started planning his music park, he'd had to fight with local officials over permits and other issues involving the project. Those disputes continued even after the park opened, and it no doubt took much of the joy out of the whole operation. Add to that situation the now intense recording of duets, and the constant trips back to Nashville studios, and you come up against a decision.

Finally, between career and park issues, Mom and Dad opted to move back to Music City in 1972.

They sold the country music park, and we moved back to Nashville. We lived on Tyne Boulevard for a short time, and then moved to a big house on Franklin Road. They'd spent a fortune on building the country music park in Florida, and on returning to Nashville, the money kept flowing both ways, in and out.

I can't even imagine what the decorating and landscaping costs were when they started working on the Franklin Road house. And that was above and beyond all their gifts and toys for each other!

They had a houseboat that they docked out at Old Hickory Lake. Dad named it *The First Lady*. Ralph Emery tells a great story about those days. This involves Mom and her longtime friend country star Jan Howard. Mom called her by her given name, Lula Grace. It is also one of the few times I've ever known of Mom playing the "star card."

Mom and Dad loved to spend time on that houseboat. Non–show business, socially elite Nashvillians owned most of the luxury boats anchored in the area, and Mom usually loved being just a face in the crowd for the frequent cookouts. The problem was, in the entire lake crowd, there were only two nondrinkers: Mom and Jan.

Dad liked it that way. He did not like seeing Mom drink. Several times out on the road she tried to fake that she was drinking heavily just to teach him a lesson. But he soon figured out that the band members were watering down her drinks to the point they had no effect.

So out on the lake, Mom and Jan were the only reliably sober people, and as such were relegated to kitchen duty. At first, Mom enjoyed feeding the crowd. It was a welcome switch from being on the road, where she often missed cooking so badly that she went to favorite fans' homes and whipped up a batch of ham and dumplings or beans and corn bread. But as time went by, the thrill wore thin, with Mom and Jan feeling like hired help. Finally, in the midst of unloading groceries she'd brought to the lake, Mom turned to Jan:

"Why are we doing this, Lula Grace? We're stars!"

They left the bags on the counter, drove to nearby Madison, Tennessee, for dinner, and left the drunks to their own devices.

The marriage of George and Tammy was already on its last shaky legs by the time Mom and Lula Grace drove to Madison for dinner.

The nippin' wasn't going to stop, and neither was the naggin'.

Dad says that his drinking was by no means the only problem they had during their marriage. The naggin' was a real problem for him, not just a funny line. He says he started feeling smothered during his marriage to Mom. He has pointed to the fact that Mom always wanted to know where he was, what he was doing, and what he was *thinking* about doing.

You only have to look at the way MeeMaw and PeePaw lived to see where Mom's marriage model came from. Mildred and Foy Lee were married for forty-two years before PeePaw passed away, and during that time they were inseparable, joined at the hip. If PeePaw needed to go to the post office, and MeeMaw was doing something else, he'd wait until she finished so they could go together. Mom thought that sounded just about perfect.

But being back in Nashville was not any sort of geographic cure. If anything, problems were exacerbated. Dad's old friend songwriter Peanut Montgomery was around a lot, and the two of them loved to drink together. They also were a creative team, though, writing "We're Gonna Hold On," one of the biggest of the duets. But Mom never quite trusted them together.

According to some, she was also jealous of Peanut's wife, Charlene, seeing her as a potential rival for Dad's heart. I never heard Mom talk about that. But I do know that she admitted that she was incredibly jealous of Dad when it came to other women. She said that she would have absolutely put her foot down if he wanted to record any duets with someone else. The only women she would have accepted as duet partners for Dad were the small group of artists she absolutely trusted: Loretta Lynn, Dolly Parton, or Jan Howard.

Tina recorded with Mom and Dad during the duet years, and in 1973, I made my stage debut. Mom later said that she believed right then that I would one day enter the family business, because I had her lungs and Dad's phrasing. There's an interesting aspect to Mom's own phrasing that she explained to Ralph Emery one time.

Ralph said, "One factor entering into Tammy's amazing vocal abilities has been completely ignored over the years. Her maternal grandmother often led what was known as old harp singin's, or, as Tammy dubbed them, fa so la singin's. These were all-day affairs where singers only sang notes, never words, relying strictly on the voice. This is in part why melodies were so important to Tammy; she could separate herself from the lyric content."

At the age of three, though, I wasn't singing Mom's songs. I was singing Tanya Tucker's debut hit, "Delta Dawn." Mom said I belted it out, even when I was little more than a toddler.

Life was never better, as far as us kids knew, as when we were living right there on Franklin Road with Tammy and George.

Eight

BECAUSE BOTH MOM AND DAD were on the road so much, and they covered up their fights, it took a long time for my sisters and me to realize that something had gone terribly wrong. In addition to their touring together, we were used to Dad being gone a lot—in some ways he was like a truck driver who spent weeks away at work, finally popping in with laughs and gifts.

Mom didn't talk about it to us, but by the time I was four years old, a divorce was in the works. What it would mean to us wasn't immediately apparent. We still had our grandparents living in the neighborhood and nannies for the times we needed full-time care.

Plus, living in that Franklin Road house was like being in a fairy tale. There was so much to do you could easily be out of touch with any real-life problems. The house had twelve bedrooms, fifteen bathrooms, and an Olympic-sized pool. The grounds were much like a paradise for kids, with a waterfall beside a big, cavelike hole, and every sort of playground equipment imaginable. There were several seesaws, a big merry-go-round, two swing sets, and a large patio with swinging chairs and a barbecue.

There was a secret room in that house, a door no one would ever notice leading into a closet, which in turn had another door leading to a small room. Mom showed it to me and said I could have it as my own personal "place." I loved that room! I loved having a secret place I could take my dolls or books or whatever I wanted, and no one could find me. Except Mom, of course, who always knew where to look for me.

I was an easygoing youngster, one who seldom got into trouble or took chances. I suppose part of that came from the fact that there was just so much to do, so many types of playground equipment and diversions everywhere. But I wasn't perfect by any means, with some amount of childish behavior. I'd whine to get my way and try to hide from people if I was in the mood to pout. Of course, hiding went nowhere, since Mom had given me the secret room in the first place. My sisters were the ones who had getting into trouble fine-tuned. One of their favorite tricks was to climb on top of the house and jump down into the swimming pool. I tried to do it a few times, but I was too chickenhearted.

I ran away to the waterfall one time, feeling put upon for some reason—probably doing my chores. When I announced my plans to Mom, she played along with it, packing me a sandwich and snacks, which she put in a "hobo sack" tied to a stick. I sat out there until it started getting dark, ate my snacks, and then decided that running away to a hole in the yard wasn't as much fun as I'd thought.

Nor were Mom and Dad having much fun by 1974. For one thing, Dad's heart was broken when, on April 13 of that year, his mother, Clara, died.

Dad still tended to go off with friends like Peanut Montgomery, drinking and running around the country. Mom not only hated the drinking, but she got more convinced that they were probably running around with women out on the road. She'd been around enough country stars to know about the groupie scene.

As time went by, and neither would give, Mom came to believe that they could live together no longer. She made the decision. I don't think Dad ever would have pulled the plug. Mom saw the move from Tyne Boulevard to Franklin Road as a final attempt to save the two of them, and it hadn't worked. She hated admitting that she was calling it quits, though. It weighed on her mind that people believed in them as a couple. She knew that in a way, they were letting down the fans that loved the idea of them together, loved the duets, the tours, and the image. She continued to deny that a divorce might be in the works all through 1974, even after she was sure it was coming.

In the end, nobody in the marriage made in Honkytonk Heaven was "joined at the hip" like MeeMaw and PeePaw had been. Mom filed for divorce on January 8, 1975. It was finalized on March 21.

My sisters and I weren't sure what had happened. Sometimes I don't think Mom and Dad were, either.

• • •

I BEGAN DIVIDING my time between Mom's house and my grandparents' home on Burton Valley Road in Nashville. My sisters were old enough that Mom felt comfortable leaving them with nannies and housekeepers. Gwen was sixteen, Jackie was fifteen, and Tina was twelve. But since I was so young, she believed that unless I was with her, I'd be better off with her parents when she was on the road.

By the time I started school, I thought of MeeMaw and PeePaw's house as home. Like Mom had done with her grandparents, as well as with Mildred and Foy Lee, I began to shape my visions of the perfect marriage after that of MeeMaw and PeePaw.

The only time I know of that MeeMaw and PeePaw had any differences in their wedded life was when PeePaw made that short-lived run at being a drinker. It's a good thing that drinking wasn't very important to him, because MeeMaw wouldn't abide it. So she put her foot down, and he got off of the fast track before he really got any speed up.

MeeMaw was a night owl, staying up reading until two or three in the morning. PeePaw was one who needed to be in bed by nine o'clock. So they ended up having separate bedrooms so MeeMaw could sleep a little later in the morning and PeePaw could get to sleep at night. When they decided to make that arrangement, MeeMaw told me that their relationship was so close that they didn't need to sleep in the same bed. "We don't have to prove how much we love each other," she told me once. "And at this age, we need sleep!"

PeePaw was a quiet man, but at the same time, when he spoke, you wanted to listen. For one thing, he had a dry wit, and you didn't want to miss anything. I never heard him say a bad word about anyone. He had an easygoing nature, and I never once saw him get angry. He adored MeeMaw, who was his opposite when it came to talking. She talked all the time. PeePaw saw his job as the listener, not a "put-upon" listener, but an interested one. He wanted to know what she thought and what she had to say. Talk about a perfect husband! (It was such a great marriage that I almost think it screwed me up. I had very high expectations.)

They split up their household duties into the areas they liked. MeeMaw liked paying the bills, being the organizer, while PeePaw loved taking care of the yard, doing the gardening, even taking out the garbage. There was only one time that I know of that they had a slight disagreement about this division of duties. MeeMaw had been quite sick in 1984, and after she got better, she started worrying that PeePaw wouldn't know what to do businesswise if she died. She explained to me that she had tried to have a conversation about insurance papers and safety-deposit boxes. He wouldn't even talk about it.

"Now, Foy, you've got to—"

"Stop this right now," he said. "I don't want to hear this." It was the only time I'd ever heard of him interrupting her.

MeeMaw almost got tears in her eyes when she told me what he'd said next.

"Your PeePaw is so sweet, Georgette. He told me that the reason he didn't want to hear anything about our business was that it was irrelevant. If I died, he wouldn't last a day."

PeePaw never had to test that theory, because he was the first to go. But I think that even if he'd lived through the shock of her death, he would have been a shell of himself from that day forward.

I saw PeePaw cry only once. I'm sure there were other times he had tears in his eyes, but in his world, men didn't cry, so he tried to hide his emotions. The time he couldn't keep it from me happened because of his overwhelming love for his grandchildren. Gwen had grown up, was living in Colorado, and was coming home just for sporadic visits. Being the first grandchild, Gwen was extra special to MeeMaw and PeePaw, and I knew they hated her long absences. Once, after she'd left to drive back to Colorado, I happened to go downstairs and overhear soft sobs coming from PeePaw's bedroom. I peeked in, and he was standing there, his shoulders shaking. I knew how he'd have hated me seeing him in a weak moment, so I quietly left. But I knew what it was about. I'd seen the look on his face when Gwen pulled out of the drive.

Maybe that's why he seemed to try to keep me a child for so long. MeeMaw used to laugh that he still tried to pick me up when I was a twelve-year-old! She'd say, "Foy, you can't carry that girl around! Her feet are draggin' the ground!" He'd just smile and say, "But, Mildred, she wants me to pick her up!"

MeeMaw and PeePaw are part of the reason I think I never really felt threatened by Mom's career. Sure, it took her away a lot, but there was a close family right there to fill in. And boy, did they ever do that up in style. I don't mean money-style, either. They didn't lavish gifts on people, although we certainly got our share on special occasions. With MeeMaw and PeePaw, it was more about time and experiences than money.

They were spontaneous people. I can't even guess how many times they'd say, "Let's drive to North Carolina and go fishing." Or maybe they'd want to pack up the car and take us grandkids to a museum or an amusement park. They'd load up a basket with sandwiches and a six-pack of peach Nehi pop, and off we'd go in the early morning. They liked to stop at little country inns for breakfast, and MeeMaw always saved a few biscuits for me to eat later with butter and sugar.

I was a tomboy when I was little, preferring the out-of-doors to being in the house, games over all dolls but one. The doll I loved was named Velvet, appropriately, because that's what she was made of. I carried Velvet everywhere until finally the material was so worn that it began falling apart. MeeMaw tried her best to locate another doll like Velvet, but the line had been discontinued. When she was finally too far gone to salvage, I was back to my Stretch Armstrong action figure and Lego sets. It wasn't that I disliked "girly" pursuits, but I just liked other things more. The great thing about Mom is that she let each of us be what came natural. She didn't try to turn us into "little girls in a row" for publicity photos or that sort of thing.

When I was at Mom's house, we played games; she loved games of all kinds. She was good at them, too, especially gin rummy. I don't think I ever saw her lose at gin. The same goes for playing the slots when we were in Las Vegas. She just played the dollar slots, never anything more expensive, but she was incredibly lucky. She'd take a handful of dollars and run it up—then walk away. She had no problem calling it quits when she gambled. She was good at other games, too. She loved playing Spades or Rook, Monopoly and the game of Life. She was very competitive.

Once when we were playing Monopoly, I decided that it was one time I would win. So I started trying to cheat. She caught me and gave me a lecture, finally saying, "Cheaters never win, Georgette." So I started playing fairly again, and kept losing—until it was my turn to be the banker. Then I immediately started slipping money from the bank over to my money pile. Sure enough, I ended up winning.

"See how nice it is to win fair and square?" Mom asked.

I sat there frowning and finally answered. "I wouldn't know, because I was cheating again!"

She shook her head, but I could see that she could barely stop from laughing, no doubt wishing I hadn't gone back to the cheating side but glad I admitted it. She saw humor in so many situations.

Mel Tillis once told me that one of his favorite memories of Mom was how much she loved to laugh. And almost nothing could make Mom laugh more than Loretta Lynn stories, whether she was listening to them or telling them. She thought Loretta was one of the funniest people in the world. "Loretta couldn't tell a lie if her life depended on it," Mom loved to say. Her favorite "Loretta moment" happened at the Grand Ole Opry, during an awards show where several women shared a dressing room. That night there were four of them "rooming" together—Mom, Loretta, Barbara Mandrell, and Minnie Pearl. They were getting dressed, when suddenly Barbara realized that she had misplaced one of the new diamond earrings that her husband, Ken Dudney, had given her for their anniversary.

"Stop everything," Barbara cried out. "You've got to help me find it! Ken will be so mad if he finds out I've already lost one of those earrings!"

So everything else rolled to a halt. There were those women, half ready for their appearances, some with rollers in their hair, tearing apart the dressing room looking for Barbara's diamond earring. They tore into the mess of beauty paraphernalia and bags scattered around, took all the cushions off the couch and chairs, shook out the clothes Barbara had been wearing before she put on her gown. In the middle of the hunt, there was a knock on the door and Ken Dudney walked in.

Loretta did not hesitate, but blurted out: "Lordy, Ken! Barbara's done lost one of them new earrings!"

"Loretta!" Barbara cried out.

Loretta looked confused for a split second. Honesty is second nature to her. Then she said, "Oh, Barbara, I'm sorry! It just hit my brain and my mouth at the same time!"

Mom said she laughed so hard that she didn't know whether she'd have the strength to finish getting ready for the show.

Mom could blurt out some funny stuff herself.

Once after I was grown, when Mom was booked on the *Late Show with David Letterman,* she started getting nervous. Ironically, the very thing that kept her watching Letterman terrified her—the fact that he said absolutely anything to anyone. And he pulled no punches.

"It's funny when he does it to other people, Georgette," she said.

Mom always remained fearful right up to showtime. Her biggest worry involved her appearance. Was her hair fixed just right? What about her gown? She was married to George Richey by then, and given what happened, I guess he thought he could kid her into losing the jitters.

I was home watching it on television, and I could see how nervous she was when she first walked out. She looked beautiful in an orange strapless dress, with perfect hair and makeup. She wanted to look right up-to-date and sophisticated for a show like Letterman's. The dress was in no way too revealing, but it certainly did emphasize the fact that although she was a tiny woman, she did have large breasts.

"You look great, Tammy," Letterman said, appreciatively.

Flustered, Mom pulled a Loretta and said the first thing that came into her mind.

"Well, my husband just told me I look just like a carrot with boobs."

WHEN I WAS growing up, Mom would do funny things to entertain my friends and me. She loved to turn backbends, and not just any run-of the mill backbend. Mom would put a small paper cup of water on the floor, turn a backbend until her head was right over the cup—then pick it up with her teeth and drink the water! Another trick was putting M&M's on a plate on the floor, turning a backbend, and eating the candies off the plate. She was as good as a carnival act.

Did I mention carnivals? Mom *loved* playing fairs and festivals that had carnivals attached. Mom loved the midway! She'd tie her hair back, put on a ball cap and sunglasses, and off we'd go through the maze of corn dog and cotton candy stands, the rides and the fun houses. Mom loved anything scary—the wilder the ride, the better she liked it. The more horrible the monsters, the better she loved the Tunnel of Doom. They both scared me, so she always held me close. "Don't be afraid, Georgette!"

Mom never got scared. We'd be riding through Bubba's Surprise or something, and she'd be screaming and laughing at the same time. I remember the first time we rode in the Zipper, which had little cages that spun when you pulled a handle. I kept thinking, *Don't pull that handle,* and all the while I knew very well that she'd pull it at the first opportunity. After the first time we went spinning, I started begging her to pull the handle the minute we got in the cage. She was such a big kid at those times.

There was a serious side to Mom's parenting. She believed that if you didn't teach your children to accept responsibilities around the house, they'd never be able to deal with being out on their own as adults. I learned that from her, and I've tried to put it to work in raising my twin sons. If kids can't take care of themselves, what have you taught them that is useful? Nothing. They'll have trouble in their relationships, whether it is with a friend, a roommate, or a spouse.

I hate to admit this, but I wasn't always a willing student when it came to personal responsibility. To earn my small allowance, I had to keep my room cleaned and my clothes washed, plus do some general household duties like feeding the cat. When I was about twelve, Mom said it was time to start doing my own ironing. After thinking it over, I protested.

"I don't know how to iron, Mom! Connie's the maid. She knows how to iron. Why can't she still do it?" Mom's eyes narrowed, and she sat back in her chair a little. Finally, she gave me her answer.

"Connie isn't *the maid,* Georgette. I pay her to work for me. Remember that. She works for me, not you. And you will learn to take care of your own things until you earn the money to hire someone to do it for you."

I did learn about money and turned into a bit of a negotiator—not to mention a little cheap. When I was in grade school, my allowance was seven dollars a week. I got to thinking about that seven dollars and decided I was worth more than that. So I went into Mom's office and typed out an official-sounding letter requesting a raise in salary. I mentioned that in addition to being given more chores over the past year, I was making good grades. I explained that with the extra money I could save up to buy Christmas presents and spend when we went on family outings. Mom raised my allowance to ten dollars a week.

Of course, I didn't have to use the allowance for Christmas presents in the first place, because each year Mom gave us each $300 to shop for gifts.

Mom loved Christmas. She wanted every inch of the house decorated, with people gathering for dinners and parties all through the season. We were Christmas Central. Long beyond the time when we thought there was a Santa Claus, we each had stockings. Even Mom had a stocking that the kids filled.

We got our shopping money a couple of months ahead of time so that we could take our time and really find things we thought each person would appreciate. MeeMaw would take me out shopping, and I was *very* careful with my purchases. So careful, in fact, that I spent only around sixty or seventy dollars each year.

Let's face it: I was cheap. MeeMaw always laughed about me being such a Scrooge. One time I thought I'd hit the jackpot when I found a deal on scarves—three for five dollars. I said that took care of three people, since I could give one to Mom, one to my aunt Ruby, and one to someone else, probably my aunt Carolyn. When MeeMaw questioned those less than generous gifts, I explained it all to her.

"But I have to keep enough money to put some in my savings account!"

Years later, when I had my own children, I found myself being the opposite. I'd spend my last dime on my boys, savings be damned.

Nine

THE THING THAT WENT MISSING from my world after 1975 was Dad. I saw him less and less in the years after Mom and Dad divorced. They continued to tour, the demand for duet performances never diminished by their divorce. It might have even been a side benefit, because people tended to watch them and speculate that they still loved each other but were just star-crossed. I think they did still care deeply, and that made the divorce doubly painful. It's one thing if you part company despising the other person. But when love remains, it can be gut-wrenching.

Both Mom and Dad had a hard time dealing with the divorce for several years, and seeing each other on tour didn't make things easier. They continued to bring me out during the show, but once I left the stage, I had almost no interaction with Dad. As years went by, I came to understand about divorce and parents whose feelings are still hurt. Mom hadn't really worked out any solution to when or where I spent time with Dad. And he wasn't one to push anything.

Although I didn't know it until a few years later, Dad frequently stopped by MeeMaw and PeePaw's house, usually late at night after he'd been drinking. MeeMaw said he would ask if it was all right to just sit by my bed and watch me sleep. She'd offer to awaken me, but he always said no, that he was ashamed that he was drunk. The thought of it breaks my heart.

Mom not only still cared deeply for Dad, but she was faced with what she considered yet another personal failure: a third divorce. She also had a fear of performing alone. They'd been on tour together since they got married, and the success of their duets brought fans out in droves in the early '70s.

All of those fears played on her mind, and as young as I was, I could feel the change. I finally brought it up, telling her that everything seemed to have gotten dark since Daddy went away. Mom said that those words snapped her back some, although I know she continued to hurt for a long time.

Dad was hurting, too. He threw himself into opening his second Possum Holler nightclub, this one on Printers Alley in Nashville. Printers Alley had once been the backstreet where people employed in the printing industry downtown partied. It remains a hot spot. Dad didn't own the club, but his name was on it. When he talked about that club in his own autobiography, he mentioned that people have asked him why he didn't get money handlers around him to manage his finances. The truth is, he did many times. And many times he ended up being taken by them.

I think that is why Dad plays it so close to his vest. He has been cheated enough times that he does not trust easily. And after his marriage to Mom fell apart, he really didn't trust anyone. Like Mom, he'd wanted that marriage to work.

For months after they were apart, both of them ended up talking about the other one when they appeared on Ralph Emery's television shows.

One of the stories Mom told Ralph soon after the divorce was about a time when Dad was two hours late for a show in South Louisiana—Cajun country. He was fresh off his hit "She Thinks I Still Care." When Dad jumped out of the camper in which he traveled, a big Cajun grabbed him: "Hey, George Jones. You s'posed to be up on them stage there singin' 'She Thinks I Don' Care Some No More.' "

Ralph said that Mom loved that story.

On one *Pop Goes the Country* segment after the divorce, Dad sang his hit "Her Name Is . . ." The lyric alludes to the love of the man's life while never mentioning a name. After George sang, Ralph asked him to complete the line. George grinned, ducked his head a bit, and said, "Tammy Jones."

"You could always feel the love they had for each other," Ralph says.

It has been important for me to know that Mom and Dad were in love and that I was a part of it. I think that this is something all children of divorce would like to know, that they were conceived in a loving home. We all have doubts and fears about one or both parents, about whether they miss seeing us when we are apart. Worse, we may get caught up in the battles that often follow a split. That's when children often feel that they may have caused the divorce.

OUR HOUSE ON Franklin Road was a little like an ongoing slumber party by the late 1970s. Mom surrounded herself with staff, friends, and a writer employed to help her write her memoirs. She hadn't wanted to write them.

Here's how she explained it:

"Simon and Schuster had been calling my manager, asking me to write an autobiography," she said. "I didn't want to do it, because I felt I had so much more living to do."

The publishing house persisted, and finally Mom agreed to meet with them in Nashville. "Michael Korda came to town, and I cooked dinner for him. He gave me his pitch, and I said no one more time. I explained that I'd be ready to write my life story in ten or fifteen years. Do you know what he said without skipping a beat? He said, 'Maybe ten or fifteen years from now no one will care.' What if he was right? What if nobody would remember my name in ten years? I signed on the dotted line."

I don't know if Mom ever gave a thought to what all she would tell in her book, *Stand by Your Man,* which was published in 1979. But I do know that when my dad read it, he was furious—and hurt.

• • •

MOM STARTED SEEING other men fairly soon after the divorce. None of it got past my dad. On one memorable occasion not long after their divorce, Mom was booked on Ralph Emery's television show *Pop Goes the Country.*

"Shorty Lavender was booking both Tammy and George," Ralph recalls. "Shorty called and asked me to let Jones come to the show. He came in, stood backstage just where Tammy could see him. He waved at her, made faces at her. He'd make suggestions in a big stage whisper: 'Ask her about that football player she's dating, Ralph.'"

Mom was then dating New England Patriots star Tommy Neville. Costar Larry Gatlin, not knowing of the Tommy Neville connection, thought George's comment alluded to fights over the amount of time Dad spent watching televised professional football games, and commented: "Here's a song idea for you: our marriage went to hell over Pete Rozelle."

Of course, Larry Gatlin's brother Rudy was one of her boyfriends at the time, too. I didn't know that much about Rudy Gatlin or Tommy Neville. I do have memories of the two that I consider the best and the worst. Given that I spent so much time with my grandparents, a lot of Mom's dating was out of my realm of knowledge.

The one I most recall is Burt Reynolds; he is the boyfriend—and later friend—that I consider the best of all. Mom first met him through Jerry Reed in September of 1975. Burt was in Nashville to appear on Jerry's syndicated television show and was planning a dinner with Jerry, Ray Stevens, and the show's producers. Mom was scheduled to be on the show, and Burt asked Jerry to invite her to the dinner as well. They dated off and on for a while, and Burt even convinced Mom to buy a vacation home in Jupiter, Florida, near his ranch.

I suppose they would have made a good couple if they'd decided to marry, but both seemed to shy away from the other's fame, from becoming Mr. Wynette or Mrs. Burt. Mom also said they'd probably fight over the mirror, and she'd have to watch Burt flirt with other women even as he walked down the aisle. The most important thing about that relationship is that they became good friends and continued to be close even after they no longer dated.

Later, after Mom married George Richey, I could tell that Mom's friendship with Burt drove Richey crazy, absolutely nuts. Richey especially resented it when Burt let Mom fly to various shows on his private plane. He covered up his feelings around Burt or people in the music industry, but you could hear the annoyance in his voice when Mom talked about them going to visit Burt at his home in Florida or accepting the offer of a flight to a concert. My favorite thing about going places on Burt's plane was that he always played cards with me. Like Mom, he liked to play gin rummy. But when you think about it, how many movie stars are going to treat a kid like a pal, play cards, and tell funny stories? Burt treated kids like real people. I never once felt like I was a fifth wheel or in the adults' way.

I loved going places with Burt, both when they were dating and afterward. I liked him so much that I spent a long time making him a present, a ceramic ashtray. Mom had given me a pottery-making set for Christmas that year, and the first thing I wanted to do was to make an ashtray for Burt. Mom knew I was making him something, but she didn't know exactly *what*. It was only after I presented my masterpiece to him that I realized he didn't smoke. I couldn't believe it, because he smoked in so many of his movies! But Burt kept that ashtray for years, proudly displaying it right along with priceless decorative items in his house.

I wish all my experiences with Mom's men had been so positive. The worst was her fourth husband, Michael Tomlin. Michael worked in real estate and traveled with some of Nashville's wealthy crowd. Mom admitted that he basically swept her off her feet with flowers and fancy restaurants. You would think that someone who had as many hit records and awards as she did would not be capable of falling for a smooth talker flashing around a roll of bills. But she loved being treated like a princess, so he obliged.

Mom also admitted that she may have been trying to put up a barrier between herself and the heartache she believed she would feel if she continued to see Burt Reynolds or counted on him being a long-term relationship. She didn't even want Burt to know that she was marrying this character. She also knew it was a bad idea, and she went right on with it anyway. Everyone close to her knew it was a mistake, but the one who had the actual nerve to tell her so was my dad.

It was so unlike him to meddle in someone's personal business, no matter how strongly he felt about it. He would take a stand for someone else, yet not get in the middle of their decision making. But when he heard that Mom was marrying Michael Tomlin, he phoned and told her she was making a serious mistake. She blew him off and kept right on planning her wedding. The #1 song in the nation was "Golden Ring," a George and Tammy duet.

The marriage was doomed. Mom knew she was making a terrible mistake and was on the verge of tears half the time on her wedding day, July 18, 1976. I believe that Mom's reasons for marrying Michael Tomlin are complicated. The most important person in the story is actually Burt Reynolds. Mom joked about not marrying Burt because he'd be flirting with women even as he walked down the aisle. But that wasn't just an offhand remark. She was afraid of what being married to a movie star would mean. She was terrified that she'd be hurt if she let their relationship turn serious. I think she was running from Burt and his whole world.

Once she started thinking about marrying Michael, the reasoning took another turn. Mom had never had a real wedding, with all the bells and whistles, and she *really* wanted one. She planned it right down to the orchids and foliage that turned our Franklin Road yard into a tropical paradise. Arrangements of pineapples and mangoes floated on little Styrofoam boats in the pool. And the flowers on the food table were arranged to look like a roast pig!

The next day they went to Washington, D.C., where Mom was to perform for President and Mrs. Gerald Ford. The event was packed with celebrities including Ella Fitzgerald, Roger Miller, and Elizabeth Taylor. Michael showed his lack of class by telling Mom that meeting Elizabeth Taylor had "made" his week. When Mom related the conversation to Elizabeth Taylor, who knew Mom and Michael were just married, Ms. Taylor kindly brushed off the comment by saying that it was just like a man to say something he didn't mean.

Then they went on a Hawaiian honeymoon where Michael acted surly and seemed threatened by the fact that Mom had once been Mrs. George Jones. He twisted one conversation about sandwiches into an accusation that Mom thought he was going to "fetch" food for her. And he suggested that *she* should be fetching *him* sandwiches. Mom wasn't feeling good anyway, so none of that went over very well. Mom ended up having to spend a night in a hospital because of stomach pains and was sick all the way back to California a few days later, where Michael wanted to see some of his family.

In San Francisco, he told Mom he wanted her to buy a Rolls-Royce when they got back to Nashville. She said she didn't need or want a Rolls-Royce. Then he said he'd take a Bentley. She informed him that she already had a limousine and a T-Bird. Mom said she was taken aback by his answer:

"Well, I'm certainly not going to drive that T-Bird George Jones bought you. And we're getting rid of that blue limo. It looks like something Isaac Hayes would drive."

Mom couldn't believe he'd actually said it. She'd recently played a benefit with Isaac Hayes, and Michael's comment offended her mightily.

When they arrived in Nashville, Michael invited a group of friends to go to Florida with them. The whole group went on Mom's bus and stayed a week, during which time Mom cooked the meals and cleaned up after people. That's after having just been in the hospital. When they got back to Tennessee, Mom had to be taken to the hospital and have her gallbladder removed. As soon as she was released from the hospital, it was back to Florida. Michael started drinking on the flight down and ended up shooting off guns later that night with some of his friends. Then he accused her of sneaking around to be with Burt Reynolds.

This marriage was clearly not going to work. Back in Nashville, they lived together a very short time, just long enough for me to see far more of this man than I ever wanted to see.

I was used to going to Mom's room if I awakened in the night. I was always a little afraid of waking up in a room all by myself, and Mom never minded me knocking on her door. During the short time that she was married to Michael Tomlin, it happened that I did wake up startled and run to her room. I could hear the television. She opened the door and let me in, comforted me, then went to the bathroom, leaving me sitting on the chair.

"Just a minute, honey," she said.

I don't think I interrupted anything because Mom had her gown and robe on. Michael was lying in bed, under the covers. Without the slightest warning, he stood up, walked straight past me, and changed the television channel. Then he turned and walked back to bed, not giving me so much as a glance. He was stark naked.

I froze. I had never seen a man or a boy with no clothes. Just then Mom came back from the bathroom and sat down next to me. I didn't say or do anything. I still couldn't move.

"Are you okay?" she asked.

I nodded, unable to speak. Then I got up, gave her a quick hug, and scurried out of the room and back to my own bed. I was horrified. I don't think he even paid any attention to the indecent thing he'd done. Looking back on it, I don't think he meant it to be a sexual experience. I think he was just that self-absorbed and crude. The fact that a six-year-old girl was sitting there while he paraded around naked was meaningless to him.

I never said a word to Mom; it was too embarrassing. Michael was out of the house within a few days anyway, without me adding that incident to the mix.

By comparison, George Richey seemed like a prize.

Ten

GEORGE RICHEY WAS ONE OF the first people Mom confided in when she knew her marriage to Michael Tomlin was a serious mistake and that she was going to have to swallow her pride and get out. Richey was a songwriter, musician, and producer. He and his wife, Sheila, had been friends with Mom for years. Richey since said that he fell in love with Mom as his marriage was falling apart, and that he was actually in love with her while she was dating Burt Reynolds.

"How could I compete with a movie star?" he asked one journalist years later.

I don't know if Richey would have tried to talk Mom out of marrying Michael Tomlin had he known her plans soon enough. He said he had barely heard of him when

Mom announced that she was getting married again. Richey didn't say anything and even played the piano at the wedding.

Richey had always been around, taking care of things for Mom after Dad moved out, giving her advice, filling in when Jackie needed an escort for a father-daughter event. As she always had, Mom loved the idea of a man stepping up and taking care of things. There's no doubt that Mom and Richey were good friends. But the events that I believe caused her to marry him when she did were manufactured, and questionable if not suspicious. It started one night in 1977 when Mom took us bowling, one of her favorite family outings. When we walked back into the house on Franklin Road, the first thing I heard was water flowing.

Every faucet in the house had been turned on, the carpets soaked. Mom chalked that up to vandals, but as things progressed, she knew she was a target. At one point, the house was set on fire. Another time, every mirror had a message written in red lipstick: *slut, whore, pig*. I remember asking Mom what *slut* meant. At seven years old, I'd never heard the term.

"It's an ugly word, Georgette," she said. "Don't ever use it."

Things escalated. Threats of violence were made over the phone. The police were continually at the house, and Mom felt terrorized every minute of the day. The police checked out a lot of people, to no avail. I don't know who made the threats or why.

I know that Dad had nothing to do with them. Aside from the fact that he wasn't even in town during a lot of those incidents, it wouldn't have been his style. Dad's approach was to drop out of sight, which was just what he was doing at that time. And I do know that the ugliness stopped the minute Mom agreed to marry George Richey. There were no more threats. No more craziness. No more break-ins.

I was too young to grasp this at the time, but the thing Richey promised Mom was safety. Not only could he protect her from whatever forces were lining up against the personal safety of her and her daughters, but he also could revive her career. He convinced her that with his knowledge of songwriting, producing, and business, she could relax and do the one thing she loved: sing. She didn't need to bother her head with business ever again.

I'm sure that sounded tempting. Richey was a good songwriter. He wrote Dad's hit "The Grand Tour," among other things. But he also seemed to be a good businessman. Just before they got together, he sold his publishing company to ATV for what was said to be a good profit. He had been out celebrating the publishing sale the night he stopped by the studio where Mom was recording and confessed his love for her.

He offered to take a load off her back. That probably sealed the deal: the suggestion that she could safely turn over her business to someone with experience and success.

Unfortunately, that's what she did. It wasn't that Mom was bad at business. She dealt with a lot of it when she was married to Dad. She was good at it, too. She kept a watchful eye on where the money went and what they needed to bring in from their concert schedule.

I've often thought about how unromantic the whole thing was: "I'll protect you and get the career back on track."

There was another element to Mom's willingness to marry someone who offered to be in charge. A dark force had been growing in her world for several years, and it would eventually destroy her: prescription drugs.

Not long after I was born, Mom had an appendectomy and a hysterectomy, the first of many surgeries. Her stomach started producing a large amount of internal scar tissue, which Mom called "floating adhesions." Because the adhesions left her in constant pain, she started taking medication. That in turn slowed down her bowel functions. Finally, more surgery was done to remove the scar tissue. More scar tissue grew, this time even larger in mass than after the hysterectomy. Another surgery. Mom saw doctors who prescribed more pain medication. It was a vicious circle that rolled right over her.

I don't believe Mom was a drug addict by popular definition. By that, I mean that she never used drugs for recreational purposes. It was never, *Let's go party and get crazy.* Mom wasn't a partyer on any level. She had real physical problems that caused serious pain, and she used increasingly more medication to quit hurting. Over the years, she did become physically addicted, a dependency that is far different from psychological or emotional addiction.

Mom was of a generation and background that seldom questioned doctors. She simply went to a doctor, was told to take a certain medication, and she did. She didn't ask questions, just took the pills. Mom saw "drugs" as something people bought from sinister-looking guys hanging out in alleys, not a man with a stethoscope and a medical degree hanging on his wall. Following surgery, most people take their pain medicine with maybe one refill, and then it's no longer needed. But even as Mom was going through the pills, more scar tissue was forming, and finally, more surgery was required. More surgery, more scar tissue, more pain pills.

Things have changed over the years. Doctors now pay close attention to what they are prescribing and what the ramifications might be. For one thing, they have to be concerned about losing their licenses. But they also know so much more about pain management. They don't prescribe in the same way. Care is taken so that what is being prescribed doesn't complicate the original physical issue.

But at the time Mom married George Richey in July of 1978, she only knew that she had health issues that caused pain and often required surgery. She also knew that prescription pain pills helped her get through days when she hurt so bad she couldn't stand it. After years of nursing, I'm never surprised when people in pain will do just about anything to make it stop.

PART THREE

Coming of Age

ELEVEN

MY SISTERS AND I LIKED George Richey when he first came into our lives. He seemed to take an interest in us and to take good care of Mom. During the years when he was known to us strictly as a friend and business colleague, Richey could not have been sweeter to Mom's daughters. As I mentioned, when Jackie needed a man to escort her to a father-daughter event, Richey volunteered. When Mom needed anything, he was Johnny-on-the-spot. That meant a lot to us.

It would be several years before we saw another side of the man, and even then, we tended to overlook it. To us and to others, he spoke of Mom in worshipful terms, and it was difficult for us to distinguish reality from illusion. Her friends were not so easily fooled. I know now that several of them questioned her marriage from the beginning and that Mom was apprehensive as well.

Mom had been heavily sedated with Demerol on July 6, 1978, the day she married Richey. Some of Mom's friends said that she had taken so much pain medication that PeePaw nearly had to carry her down the aisle. And according to at least one friend, George Richey was the one who helped her inject the Demerol.

The ceremony was held on the beach at her Jupiter Beach property. Mom's aunt Carolyn Jetton was matron of honor. Carolyn had only recently been diagnosed with liver cancer, and it was one of the hardest things my mother ever had to face—that her beloved aunt and friend was going to die.

Carolyn joked that she'd spoil the wedding photos because her chemo treatments were making her hair fall out. Mom got her a wig, and as sick as she was, Carolyn still treated it lightly. She told Mom that she believed the wig was better than her original hair anyway. My memories of Aunt Carolyn all involved a smile or a laugh. She kept a positive outlook right to the end.

A few months after their 1978 wedding, Mom and Richey went to visit Carolyn in Mississippi. They left, but when they flew into the Atlanta airport, Mom suddenly freaked out.

"We've got to go back," Mom said.

"Why?" Richey asked. "We just left!"

"I mean it, Richey! We've got to go back right now! Carolyn is dying. I can feel her going. We can make it."

They probably could have. But what they didn't count on was a two-hour flight delay. By the time they got another flight and made it back to Mississippi, Carolyn had been dead for two hours.

Although Mom sometimes got those strange feelings about impending tragedy, she never called herself "psychic" or suggested that she could foretell the future. But she sometimes had dreams that caused her to worry about a relative or a friend, and she was usually right to worry. I think in most cases, dreams are just what people say they are: a release of the subconscious. Sometimes, either by sheer coincidence or innate worries, an event from the dream may "come true" in your life.

On the other hand, I do think that some people are so much in touch with themselves that they have a gift for seeing things that go right by most of us. And I think that when it came to her loved ones, Mom was one of those people. It seemed to show up most when those she loved were dying.

She had those same thoughts about her mother in 1991. MeeMaw's health had been worsening since 1989, when she had bypass surgery. Mom moved MeeMaw to her house on Franklin Road, took care of her, and nearly went nuts every time MeeMaw had a setback. (Everything was complicated because MeeMaw had severe diabetes.) By the time of her death, MeeMaw didn't even recognize family members. That was very hard for Mom to take, but she hoped that at least when the end came, there would be some recognition. Each time she left to play a show, she feared that MeeMaw would die before she got home.

Mom's forebodings started on the road home from a show. She was nervous for the last couple of hours, checking her watch and telling the bus driver to hurry. She had no appointments, no reason in particular to be hurrying. When the bus pulled into the drive and parked by the door, Mom didn't even grab her purse, just ran into the house. MeeMaw had waited for her. Once she saw that Mom was by her side, she breathed her last.

But while Mom sometimes got little warnings that something was going wrong in the life of someone she loved, she could be dangerously out of touch when it came to her own life. Her final marriage, it seems, was a battle for control—a battle she ultimately lost. For me, there remains a big question mark over George Richey, his motivations, and his actions throughout the marriage.

Before they were married, it appeared that Richey might be a responsible person when it came to Mom's pain medication. She had overdosed a few years earlier, while she was in physical pain from her adhesions and still hurting emotionally over the divorce from Dad. Richey allegedly warned Mom about excessive use of Demerol while visiting her in the hospital, yet he was soon a part of the problem.

Even before they married, Richey started removing people from Mom's inner circle, close female friends who might have been able to get her off that destructive course. I think of this time period as the Great Divide.

Mom had surrounded herself with women she liked and trusted, friends such as her hairdresser, Jan Smith, and her memoir collaborator, Joan Dew. And there was another in whom Mom had complete trust: our nanny, Cathye Leshay. Of the various nannies we had over the years, she was my favorite. She was already a teacher when we met.

All my early schooling was in Nashville. After attending Glen Levin for preschool and kindergarten, I started first grade at St. Paul's Christian Academy, where Tina was enrolled. It was there that Joan Dew, Mom's autobiographer, found Cathye Leshay, introducing her to the household while Mom was on a road trip. Once Mom got back and realized how much we all loved Cathye, she hired her away from the school—at twice the salary. I loved and trusted Cathye. She was like a member of the family—fun to be around, yet a disciplinarian and a good tutor. Tina and I both benefited a lot from the time she spent with us. But it didn't seem to matter that Cathye had been so important to our family, she was one of the first people out the door.

One friend after another was put at a distance. It was particularly ugly in Cathye's case. She had given up a job and her own apartment to come take care of our family. The day Richey told her to leave, he said it was so that he and Mom could spend time just with each other. Funny how that worked: the minute he got Mom's entourage moved out, he started moving his own family in.

For example, my grandparents suddenly decided to move away, and Richey hired his sister and her husband to move into Mom's house and look after Tina and me. I didn't know it at the time, but it turned out that MeeMaw and PeePaw were replaced as my caretakers, and only then did they make the decision to leave Nashville, not the other way around. Richey had convinced Mom that I was being spoiled by my grandparents and that they should be replaced. It was with hurt feelings that they headed back to Alabama.

Richey and my dad were polar opposites. Dad encouraged everybody to move close to us—the more the merrier.

Billy Sherrill was gone as her producer by 1980. Neither Billy nor Mom mentioned Richey in that decision, but I find it almost impossible to believe that Mom turned to another producer without pressure from Richey. It's true that she hadn't had solo hits in a while, but I don't think that she'd have found a new producer. I think she'd have looked harder for songs. If you look at her hit-making career, when Mom had Billy in her corner, she either wrote or found hits. Once he was gone, not so much.

More than a few in Nashville felt the same way—that Richey had been waiting for the opportunity to have complete power over her career, including record production. Richey told people that was not so, proven supposedly by the fact that another producer came in for an album when Billy left. But that didn't last long. Richey was soon at the helm, and the singles did no better. Part of that involved the times. The business was in a state of flux, and many established artists scrambled to find a new niche. The removal of Billy Sherrill—even though they remained friends—was one more decision that isolated her.

I've asked myself how Mom could allow that to happen, how someone could turn her whole life around, change the way she did business. Giving Cathye her walking papers with no advance announcement was an unthinking move, unlike the "old" Mom, who was intensely concerned about the well-being of her friends and family. But once Richey was in our home, he was running it. That is something I saw repeatedly, even when I wasn't old enough or suspicious enough to understand that he was taking charge.

Up until around the time Mom married Richey, she was the spunkiest woman you'd ever meet. She'd tell anyone who tried to push her around to go jump off a bridge. She was a strong-willed woman who let people know where she stood. And if you were her friend, and you were in trouble, she was *there*. She could be intense and involved, whether it was her business or not.

But between her increasing pain and her belief that she needed to find a man she could depend on, she began making mistakes. Along came the marriage to Michael, which turned out to be a humiliating fiasco. Finally, along came the terrorizing and menacing threats not just aimed at Mom but to us girls and even her parents. That introduced a new element: physical fear. I believe that's the time her personality really started to change.

It didn't happen overnight, and it certainly wasn't a 24/7 thing. There were long periods of time when she seemed like her old self—the Tammy who could sink hook shots continued to show up almost up until the day she died. And that is why I refuse to pigeonhole Mom as some kind of eternally tragic figure.

Early on, she often stood up to Richey. I remember one time before they were married that she put him off the bus. We'd been in Las Vegas, where Richey had been throwing his weight around, and Mom got fed up.

"Get off my bus," she said. And off he got! Mom had the driver take off down the road, but within minutes, she asked that the bus be turned around to go back for him. Down the road, though, that pattern became problematic, the times when Mom would make a stand only to back down and turn the bus around.

The case of Richey and Mom's relationship is at once simple and complicated when it comes to his power issues. It is simple, because a manager always wants to exert some control over his/her client, and complicated, because they were also married and her health was precarious.

Often the reason a domineering person distances their spouse from friends and allies is that they are abusive. They know that side of themselves, and they don't want any witnesses around. I know that Richey was verbally abusive to Mom because I witnessed it myself. But I believe that he was also physically abusive. The famous "Tammy Wynette Kidnapping" story is a case in point. It happened on October 4, 1978, four months after Mom and Richey were married. It's an old and well-known tale. Mom showed up at a farmhouse near Franklin, Tennessee, badly beaten, the apparent victim of a carjacking/robbery that turned horribly violent.

More than a few people questioned the story, some assuming it was a publicity stunt, others thinking Mom had simply gone a little crazy. Years later, she would tell Jackie that the whole story was invented to hide the fact that Richey had beaten her up. Her bruises had been so bad, and so visible, that Richey knew she couldn't hide them. And so he convinced her to concoct that story.

That Tammy Wynette—the one who would agree to a convoluted cover-up and otherwise acquiesce—was a rarity during the very early years of marriage to Richey. We saw the "old Mom" more often than not. She still spoke her mind, played Monopoly and gin rummy, took us bowling, and when playing a fair or festival, put on her ball cap and rode the wild rides. She also stepped up to the plate for her friends. I've heard the stories dozens of times. I'd like to add a few of them as a balance of sorts to some of those where she caved to Richey's finagling.

Mom's dear friend Jan Howard joined the tour in 1979, after Mom realized Jan was going through an emotional low point. Jan says that being on the road with us helped her through some rough times, that she'd been on the verge of quitting music altogether. I'm sure Mom did want to help Jan, but I am equally sure that Mom loved having Jan along. Here's how Jan recalled it:

"I had very serious surgery in 1979 and decided to retire from the business. I hadn't had a hit since 1971 and had just lost the will to continue. Tammy wouldn't hear of it. She was set to go on a major European tour, and both Tammy and Richey [her husband-manager] insisted I come along. Sometimes we sang together. Sometimes I sang backup for Tammy during her solo show, and at other times, I performed some of my own songs, with Tammy—who was one of the biggest names in the music world—singing backup for me!

"Once, when we both had colds, our noses started running while we were singing a duet. Both of us were trying to wipe our noses on the microphone, and we started laughing so hard we couldn't sing. Richey stood in the wings hopping mad, but we couldn't do anything but laugh."

Therein lies the reason that whatever good Mom's invitation did for Jan's emotional well-being, Jan repaid it in spades. You see, she was one of the few who had absolutely no fear of George Richey. He seemed to know that and gave her great latitude.

Mom also stepped in when Loretta Lynn's mother passed away, leaving Loretta devastated. Mom, in fragile health, wearing spike heels, literally climbed a mountain to stand by Loretta. And it is to Richey's credit that he climbed right along with her.

"Loretta is very important to me, and I wanted to be with her during that time," Mom later explained. "I felt she needed a friend from her own industry. I knew if it had been my mother, I'd want Loretta with me no matter what. The problem was, you couldn't get to the ceremony by car. The only way up that mountain was on foot.

"After the service, we all went over to someone's house and sat around talking about Clara, Loretta's mother. Then Richey started playing the piano, and Loretta started singing old-time gospel songs. She was singing things like 'If I Could Hear My Mother Pray Again,' and we must have sung every hymn we knew by the end of the night. It was almost like we were holding a service in a Baptist church. It helped Loretta, and it helped Richey and me, too."

Mom didn't just step up to the plate for her longtime friends. She believed in offering friendship and support for newer artists, especially if she sensed in them the insecurities she'd felt when she came to Nashville. A few years ago, I saw Mel McDaniel at the Grand Ole Opry. Mel had great hits with "Baby's Got Her Blue Jeans On," "Stand Up," and so many others.

I remembered hearing Mom talk about how much she liked Mel, but I'd never spent any time around him. When entertainment attorney Philip Lyon introduced us, Mel's eyes got moist. He put his hands on my shoulders and I could see he was trying not to cry.

"Let me tell you about your mama," he said. "When I first came to this town, I didn't know anybody or anything about how the business worked. I was so nervous when I was around other artists, even after my first single got on the charts in 1976. Then I got invited to my first big industry party, and when I walked in alone, I felt like an outcast. Nobody knew me or said anything. I kind of slunk over to the corner and stood there feeling out of place and worse by the minute. When I saw your mom standing with a group of people, I almost died! Tammy Wynette! Then she looked straight at me, smiled, and started walking across the room. I kept thinking, *No—she's not coming over here!* But she did. She introduced herself—as if I didn't know her name! But then she did the greatest thing—she said she had heard my record and really liked it.

"She was so open and nice that I admitted I didn't know anyone and felt out of place. So your mom took me by the arm and escorted me all over that party! She introduced me to everyone, told them she loved my music, and made sure I was involved in the conversations. Then afterward, every time I saw her anywhere, she always asked me what project I was working on and how things were going on the road. She was really interested. She was just the friendliest, nicest woman. Your mother was a great lady."

It meant so much to me to hear that someone else saw a side of Mom I knew so well. She wanted people to be comfortable. And if there was any way she could do it, she tried to put them at ease, to make things better for them.

Those are just some of life's snapshots of the Mom I knew best: the loyal friend, the star who cheered on hopefuls, the funny lady. The times that she seemed to be a different person were sad, and although I will share them with you, I know that pain, medication, and another person's control were behind them.

MOM'S AUTOBIOGRAPHY, *Stand by Your Man,* was released in 1979. A television movie starring Annette O'Toole and Tim McIntire was released in 1981. It would be years before I understood just how badly the book and movie hurt my dad and damaged my relationship with him. Mom told stories and talked of events Dad not only didn't remember, but also didn't believe ever happened in the first place. He was more than angry. He was hurt. And we all know what George Jones does in times like that. He goes underground.

I saw Dad once not long before Mom's book came out. He was living in Alabama at the time and drove to Nashville to pick me up for a visit. I think I learned more about Dad on that trip back to Alabama than I had ever known.

You miss out on so many things when one parent is absent. Until we started off on a road trip to Alabama, I didn't know that my dad thinks beef jerky is one of the best snacks in the world. Maybe that sounds silly, but I just loved learning it. I liked knowing that another of his food passions is a bag of Krystal burgers. I remember thinking: *I love beef jerky, too, just like my dad! I love Krystals, too, just like my dad!*

Then the book was published.

I didn't see him for a long time after the trip to Alabama, and there was never any talk around home of his being mad about his portrayal in the book. Mom never said anything negative about Dad to me. What little I knew about any issues was picked up from snippets of overheard conversations between Mom and Richey. I heard that he had stopped paying child support for me. I heard that he never called to ask about me.

On the other hand, Mom always spoke highly of Dad to me. If I saw something in a tabloid or heard something from some band member, she quickly brushed it aside.

"Don't you believe any of that, Georgette. Your dad drinks too much, but he's a good man. Don't forget that."

She loved to talk about some of the bighearted things she'd seen him do, like the time he gave a piece of expensive property to one of Mom's friends who wanted to build a home, or when he had mowed her girlfriends' lawns just to help out. Why, then, I wondered, did this bighearted man so seldom want to see his daughter? Yet even as I questioned his feelings about me, I wouldn't give up hope that somehow he would be back in our lives despite this latest marriage of Mom's.

Of course, life around our house was pretty crazy then. Events were definitely weird in the late '70s, with terrorizing, an embarrassing fourth marriage, and a fifth marriage that she privately questioned and publicly praised, all topped off with a kidnapping scandal. I sometimes wonder if all the drama made Mom start wanting to distance herself from Nashville again, much like she'd done when people were gossiping about her and Dad right after they got together.

When I was in middle school, we moved from Franklin Road in Nashville to Hendersonville, still close to the business, but not in the thick of it. The house was just down the street from Johnny Cash and had once been owned by Roy Orbison. Mom decided to rehire Cathye Leshay. Cathye, it turned out, had been having a great time. She'd spent two years with a friend living on the island of Maui before returning to her home state of Alabama. Mom's attitude seemed to be that Cathye had left us to go on some grand adventure, not that she'd been let go. That's just one of the many times I believe she had no idea of how her business was conducted.

TWELVE

MY PARENTS' RELATIONSHIP WAS BOOKENDED with two of the biggest songs in country music history: "Stand by Your Man" and "He Stopped Loving Her Today." Mom and Dad questioned the wisdom of releasing both of these classics, yet the records went on to capture the hearts of country fans throughout the world. Mom's signature song happened early in her career, Dad's was considered a comeback.

Neither Mom nor Dad had many high-impact solo hits during the years their duets were topping the charts and they were winning Duo of the Year awards. Dad's biggest solo hits during that time were "Her Name Is . . ." in 1976 and "Bartender's Blues" in 1978. After Mom's #1 in 1976, "You and Me," her highest-charting single was "Womanhood" in 1978. In 1981, she didn't even break into the Top Twenty with "Cowboys Don't Shoot Straight (Like They Used To)." It was the lowest she'd charted since her debut single, 1966's "Apartment Number Nine."

I'm sure it was a bitter experience for Mom, not to mention Richey, who was by then her manager and career guru. While Mom struggled to find a hit, Dad had something—if not up his sleeve, then in his pocket.

He just didn't know it.

Dad's life had gone from bad to worse since the divorce. He got into business with people who cheated him; he went broke and nearly ended up homeless. One of the biggest problems involved land investments. Dad does have a good eye for property. He always has been able to spot a good land deal. But to make that translate into profit, somebody *trustworthy* has to act as the manager. Dad bought properties, then got bored, and too often sold at a loss. As the money drained away, he drank more.

Dad has a love-hate relationship with money—just as he does with stardom. He likes the comfort money brings, but there is something about "riches" that is off-putting to him. There's an old story about him that illustrates his feelings about money and about putting personal wealth above all else. During his post-divorce, pre–Nancy Jones days, Dad got to talking with Webb Pierce. Both of them had no doubt been drinking. Those who knew Webb well will tell you that he could be overbearing at times, to say the least. Webb was going on about how rich he was, and Dad finally told Webb he'd thrown away more money than Webb ever made. Then Dad pulled a wad of bills out of his pocket and started flushing them down the toilet. Sure, it's an alcohol-fueled story—but it also speaks worlds about George Jones's attitude toward money.

He had friends who helped him. The mid to late 1970s were dominated by outlaw country music, and Waylon and Willie were tearing up the charts. Waylon considered Dad one of his musical heroes. He said, "If we could all sing like we'd want to, we'd all sing like George Jones." And he was one of the friends who came to Dad's rescue, leading to an incident that became one of songwriter Mickey Newbury's favorite George Jones stories.

It seemed that Mickey was in Nashville pitching songs and happened to see Dad pull his car up in front of the Spence Manor Hotel on Sixteenth Avenue. Mickey said that Dad got out and walked toward the Spence, leaving the car door wide open. Mickey was on foot, and by the time he got to the car, Dad was already inside the Spence. When Mickey started to close the door for Dad, a paper bag fell out, spilling bundles of cash on the pavement. It looked like a *lot* of money.

Thank goodness, Mickey was as honest—and as blasé about money—as Dad. He put the bundles of cash back in the bag and went in the Spence. When he finally found the right room, Dad looked at the bag and simply said, "Oh yeah. Waylon gave me that." It turned out to be around forty thousand dollars.

Mickey (who passed away in 2002) was known to tell people that he'd once been George Jones's bagman.

Dad appeared to have been in desperate circumstances for several years. But as I mentioned, he'd been carrying something important around in his pocket: a song.

Billy Sherrill had tried for quite a while to convince Dad that "He Stopped Loving Her Today" (written by Bobby Braddock and Curly Putman) was a hit. Dad thought the song needed something—another verse, a bridge, *something*. But Billy was already on that case. He'd asked Braddock and Putman to rewrite the song. They tried several versions and added the recitation before Billy thought it was *there*. He made Dad listen again.

This time Dad agreed that the song was finished, but he thought it was so depressing that fans would reject it. Worse, he worried that people would say it was about Mom and that he was feeling sorry for himself. But he stuck the cassette tape in his pocket and carried it around with him.

Billy bet him a hundred dollars that fans would love it, and Dad finally agreed to include it on his next album. The only question then was whether Dad ever actually would sing it. Dad was so disinterested that he put off sessions, and when he did show up, would often start singing Kris Kristofferson's "Help Me Make It Through the Night." It was only because of Billy Sherrill's tenacity that "He Stopped Loving Her Today" was finished, recorded, and released in April of 1980.

It goes without saying that Dad lost the hundred-dollar bet. And knowing that a song of this stature had such shaky beginnings should reassure songwriters.

Music careers are often much like those wild rides Mom loved. You can go from the bars of East Texas to a limo in Nashville, back down to living in a car, then back to limos and awards-show red carpets. As they say on Music Row, it all begins with a song.

"He Stopped Loving Her Today" gave Dad his first

platinum album, *I Am What I Am,* and more awards than he'd ever seen. The song won a Grammy and was named Single of the Year by both the Country Music Association and the Academy of Country Music. Both organizations also named Dad Male Vocalist of the Year. Amazingly, it was named the CMA Song of the Year twice, in both 1980 and 1981, with that honor bestowed by the ACM in 1980.

Dad was clearly on a roll, the toast of Nashville. And as usual, when things were going well, Dad was out and about more. I did get to see him briefly from time to time, but not as often as I'd have liked.

Then one night when I was ten years old, Dad sent word that he hoped to see me when Mom played the Opry. I was so excited because it had been months since we'd had any contact. Mom booked us a room at the Opryland Hotel, and we waited. Time passed, and I sat there waiting. When Mom finally told me it was time to go to the show, I refused to leave. Daddy was coming to see me! Mom agreed to let me stay with one of her assistants until he arrived, but No-Show Jones lived up to his name that night.

It wasn't the first time Dad had left me waiting, but cooling my heels there at the Opryland Hotel, with Mom's assistant watching me with a pitying look, devastated me. Mom said she was sorry that Dad hadn't been able to make it, that she didn't know what had happened. I honestly don't think she knew.

Soon after that incident, Mom and Dad started doing a lot of work together. Still, he made no effort to see me. The few times our paths crossed, he didn't have much to say. I started thinking that maybe because he was back on top of the country music heap he thought I was a big drag. I didn't know. I made no effort to find out anything from him, nor did I speak of it to Mom. I let it fester for years.

Flash forward: Some months after Mom died, when I was spending some time with Dad and his wife, the former Nancy Sepulveda, I finally brought it up. Nancy shot a quick look at Dad, and the look on her face told me that there was more to this situation than his simply blowing me off. Neither of them was surprised that I remembered that it had happened right after "He Stopped Loving Her Today" came out. They knew exactly what night I was talking about, what had happened—and why.

George Richey had determined that Dad's success meant the time had come for a George-and-Tammy music revival complete with an album and a tour. Richey told Dad that under no circumstances could he see his daughter until he agreed to the terms. Dad's reaction was typical. He just threw his hands in the air and said, "The hell with it: do the album and the tour."

Richey had used me to extort my *father.*

I didn't know about the shakedown at the time, nor would I have been able to comprehend it if I had. I couldn't quite let go of the idea that Mom and Dad would somehow get back together. It took the equivalent of a kick in the gut for me to grasp that it wasn't going to happen. The event that finally convinced me occurred not long after the time Dad was a no-show at the Opryland Hotel.

Mom and Dad had been divorced for six years. During that time, I had seen Mom date several men and marry two of them. But even though I had been present at both of Mom's post-Dad weddings, neither seemed real to me.

Michael Tomlin had been removed from my world fast enough. (Well, maybe not quite fast enough. He'd had time to gross *me* out.) But if Michael had come and gone quickly, the same could happen with Richey, or so I thought.

My dad could still come home. They could get married again, and I would have my family back. It was a dream that got harder to hang on to as Dad showed up to see me less often. But hang on I did.

Mom brought news that gave me renewed hope in 1981. Bobby Braddock had written a song titled "Daddy Come Home" with Dad and me in mind. Mom wanted me to sing it with Dad, not just onstage, but on a television show! We would perform the song on a Home Box Office special Dad was taping, for the world to see. Mom was appearing as well, singing " 'Til I Can Make It on My Own," the 1976 hit she had written with Billy Sherrill and Richey.

The three of us went together on the day of the taping, Mom, Richey, and me. I conveniently ignored the fact that Mom's fifth husband was with us. He might as well have been on the moon for all I cared. I had it all figured out. I was going to sing my heart out and bring my daddy back home. I had no way of knowing that this performance was tied directly to the time Dad didn't come to see me at the Opryland Hotel.

The minute I saw my dad, I ran to him and hugged him. *This is how it is supposed to be,* I thought. After months of not seeing my father, he was right there with me and my mom. He hugged me back and asked—with that smile I loved so—if I was ready to sing. He didn't know *how* ready I was. I'd been concentrating on the song for days, practicing both alone and in front of Mom. I believed that she had a strong reaction to the lyrics, too. They seemed to make her a little sad, and I believed the sadness meant that she still loved Daddy.

It was up to me to bring Dad on board.

I believed that if I could sing that song well enough, I could save my family. I just had to make him really listen to the words.

Daddy, come home, oh please, Daddy, come home.
Sweet Daddy, are you out there somewhere all alone?
Was Mommy mean to you, did I treat you wrong?
Daddy, oh Daddy, come home.

I did sing my heart out. I put everything I had into that song, and when I finished singing, I looked up at Daddy's face. He smiled and gave me another hug. Then Mom and Dad quickly shook hands and Mom whisked me out the door.

That was the end of it.

On the way home from the HBO taping, I sat in the backseat of the car, aching, knowing I had failed in the most important task I'd ever had. From that day on, I accepted that Mom was married to someone other than my dad and that nothing I could do would change it.

Once again, only later did I learn the reason that Dad had made no attempt to see more of me at the time. He was too often reminded that seeing me and singing with mom were connected, and he got sick of the games.

Maybe it is wishful thinking, but I question whether Mom knew what had really been behind the new George-and-Tammy tour. Everything I have heard or read about that tour suggests that it was a booker, Jim Halsey, who was behind the idea. That may be. But George Richey's brother Paul was now Dad's manager, and I suspect the brothers promised they could deliver Jones. Mom's involvement? A part of me believes she didn't have a clue. The reason I say this goes back to another incident, this one involving child support.

I'd heard Mom and Richey talk briefly about Dad not keeping up payments. But it wasn't something they often brought up, and I don't remember it being a major issue. It had been Richey who insisted to Mom that Dad pay up in the first place. As I recall, she hadn't cared about it.

Years later, I learned that Dad had tried to make a big payment, and one of his business partners had pocketed it. But neither Mom nor Richey told me about that. If Mom said anything directly to me about missing child support, it was usually just with a shrug: "We don't need it," or, "Your dad just doesn't pay attention to business." As it turned out, Mom was no longer hands-on about taking care of her business, either.

After Dad married Nancy in 1983, I did spend more time with Dad. Nancy saw to it that I did. On one of those afternoons, I went into my stepmother's office looking for Dad. As we talked, I noticed that Nancy had been writing checks. One of them stunned me. It was a child support check! I had been led to believe that my father didn't pay any support. Yet there was the check on my stepmother's desk, right next to an envelope addressed to my mom's company: "Two thousand dollars. Georgette/support."

"What is that?" I asked before I realized how impolite it sounded.

"That's child support, Georgette," Nancy answered, brushing my rudeness aside. "It's supposed to be a thousand, but your dad is trying to make up for some payments that didn't get made. He wants to make sure you have it all in your college fund before you start."

Dad walked in the room, and Nancy told him that I had been in the dark about the support checks.

"Oh yeah," he said. "I've been paying."

Something was very wrong. But the shock I felt at that moment was nothing compared to the look on Mom's face when I brought it up. One of the first things I did after I got back home and put my suitcase in my room was find my mother. I didn't waste any time about asking.

"Mom, I thought you said Dad wouldn't pay my child support."

She shook her head, looking somewhat puzzled. "Well, he doesn't. I've got plenty of money, and anyway, you know how he is about—"

"Yes, he *is* making the payments, Mom. I saw the check."

"Wh—what? A child support check?"

"Yes, Mom. I saw it. Two thousand dollars, made out to your company. It had 'Georgette/support' written on it. Nancy said Dad was trying to catch up. She said they've been making double payments for quite a while."

"Richey!" she called out to the next room. "Has George been making child support payments? Georgette says she saw one of the checks—for two thousand dollars!"

Richey walked in and shrugged. "Yeah. He's paying."

"But where's the money?"

"It goes straight into the company account," Richey said.

I don't know where I got the nerve to say this, but I did. "Nancy said the money was supposed to be for my college."

Richey gave me a withering look. "It takes a lot more than two thousand dollars a month to support you, Georgette. That money has to go into the company."

"Why didn't I know about this?" Mom asked him.

Richey shrugged again. "What difference does it make?"

Mom never said anything more about this. I don't think she even considered it a big deal or thought it made any difference. I didn't bring it up again. But knowing that Dad was trying to pay back money he had been cheated out of by a business partner did make a difference—to me.

I FINISHED MIDDLE school in Hendersonville and then transferred to Hawkins Junior High, where I almost immediately started hanging out with what Mom considered the "wrong crowd." That meant the kind of kids who thought it was cool to blow off homework, skip classes, and smoke. None of those activities sat well with Mom. She respected school and believed in getting an education. Moreover, she wanted to know where her daughters were at all times. Her mind was never at ease when she was on tour unless she could pick up a phone and find out what was going on at home.

Mom took me out of Hawkins and enrolled me at Harding Academy in Nashville, forty-five minutes from the Hendersonville house. Cathye Leshay drove me to and from school for quite a while. Then one of Cathye's friends offered her a house she owned in Nashville, so we stayed there during the school week and went back to Hendersonville on the weekends.

For a long time, I remained resentful that Mom had been so disapproving of my junior high friends. But I later understood how smart she was to have removed me from the situation. Just before I started college, I checked around to see what had happened to some of the old crowd. One girl was in jail, a boy was in the state penitentiary for drugs, and another friend had committed suicide. One of my best friends from those years was by then a sixteen-year-old mother of two, with no job and no husband, no car, no prospects. After that eye-opener, I went straight to Mom, thanked her, and apologized for my initial resentment.

"I was just watching out for you, Georgette," she said with a smile.

I'M NOT SURE what effect all the moving around during my early years had on me, and I know I wasn't unique to that experience. I do know that I sucked my thumb until I was almost ten. The only reason I gave it up was because PeePaw decided to quit smoking and I made a pact with him. He'd give up his smokes and I'd give up my thumb.

The thing that helped, that gave me a sense of stability, was that when Mom was on most of the long tours I was with her. If I wasn't going to school, I was on the road. Those were some of the greatest days, both before and after Richey came into the picture.

My parents had brought me out to meet the crowds

from the time I was a few months old. If that young experience did anything, it probably simply left me comfortable with the idea of being on a stage. It didn't seem to leave me with a burning desire to be in the spotlight. I don't even remember those early childhood show-and-tell events. My memories begin later, when Tina and I traveled with Mom as harmony singers. Tina was a wonderful singer, by the way. It always surprised me that she didn't go on to have a career in music, because she certainly had the talent.

I never thought about actually becoming an artist at the time. Back then, I was just having fun out on the road with my mother. I've mentioned Mom's love of carnivals and our fun times on the midway, but there were other fantastic times, too, sightseeing in new cities, new countries, buying books about a certain area and Mom reading them to us.

We went to England twice when I traveled with Mom, once when I was eight and another time when I was twelve. The first trip took place over Easter, and Mom arranged an Easter egg hunt at Hyde Park. What a thrill it all was: hunting eggs, watching the red double-decker buses come and go, listening to the Londoners' accents. I remember being so interested in the fact that people drove on what to me was the wrong side of the road. But the sight that attracted me most was watching the guards at Buckingham Palace. I wasn't alone in my fascination. Every adult on the tour was curious about the guards who didn't move an inch, not even to blink.

Mom had fought for me to go on the second trip. At first, the school said I could be gone for only ten days or they would hold me back for the entire year. Mom went to the principal's office and made her point: "Four extra days cannot possibly make that much of a difference. Georgette will have a tutor with her, and she will learn more about history in those two weeks than she probably would have in a whole school year. As long as she completes her assignments and passes her tests, I see no justification for either keeping her from going with me or for holding her back."

They came around to Mom's way of thinking.

Mom made sure I studied hard on that trip. I spent a lot of time reading about England, the British people, and their history. Cathye Leshay was there to tutor me, and we spent considerable time putting the travel experience to good use.

I loved the whole road trip concept, no matter if it was in Europe or just next door in Kentucky. I loved riding on the band bus, playing football, and sometimes staying up late into the night playing cards. Mom ended up hiring Dad's old band when they split up. I think they knew that Mom was going to provide a more certain income, that she wasn't going to go into hiding or miss a show. It didn't have anything to do with their feelings toward Dad, just the reality of the situation. Those band members treated me as if I were one of their own children, and I loved every one of them.

As I got a little older, Mom and I pulled pranks on each other. Sometimes we'd change the words to a song or add commentary when we were practicing, always reminding each other that we better be careful not to sing it that way onstage. We had a cool routine worked out on the song "Bedtime Story." I had appeared on the cover with her on her album, and so when we did the song onstage, she'd look back at me and smile from time to time. It's a long, involved story song that Billy Sherrill and Glenn Sutton wrote about a perfect marriage that falls apart and is put back together. The "King and Queen" in the family have a little princess they both adore, but even the perfect life doesn't compete with a woman the "King" meets with the "big, beautiful eyes." When we rehearsed the song, I'd sometimes pop up with a comment about the fact that it probably wasn't the woman's big, beautiful eyes the guy noticed first. One night I said it during a show in Canada. Mom started laughing and rolled the whole thing to a stop.

"I'm sorry for losing it, but my daughter just cracked me up," she said to the audience. "We'll start over."

"Sorry!" I said.

"No, no," Mom said, still laughing. "It was funny!"

I saw Dad a little more following "He Stopped Loving Her Today," after Mom and Dad started working together. But the meetings often seemed forced, which, of course, they *were*! It took me a long time to figure that there was another problem.

I had started looking more and more like Mom.

Even though it made me feel sad, it was important for me to know that so often when he looked at me, my father saw my mother, remembering all the good—and the bad—times. Old resentments were brought to the surface. I now see that the times I talked on and on about Mom were hurtful to Dad. That never once occurred to me. Back then, all I saw was that he was getting short-tempered and irritable. With that misunderstanding going on, we were unable to build a real relationship. His marriage to Mom always stood in the middle. There was competition as well as resentment.

"Mama took us to Hollywood with her, Daddy! We got to shop, and I got a swimsuit. Tina got these cool shoes. I've got some pictures of us!"

My father would nod, glance at the pictures, and then brush me off. I took that to mean he had no interest in me or my life. Little by little, I stopped telling him what I did, what I cared about, what I feared, what I loved.

THIRTEEN

AS YOU MIGHT EXPECT AFTER reading about the child support checks, the tone of our family reunions took a distinct upturn once Nancy Sepulveda married my dad. Nobody is more "tell it like it is" than she.

Nancy encouraged Dad to stay in better touch with me and to let me know what was going on in his life. There were still times that we lost touch, especially after I was in my twenties. But Nancy tried. She also wanted to facilitate some kind of peace between my mom and dad, especially if they were going to be working together.

I will go on record right here and say that my stepmother is a saint. If I had scripted the perfect stepmother, she would be the one. She's strong without being hard, and she's the ultimate caregiver. If Nancy sees someone in need, she reaches out to them and doesn't give up. That made her the perfect woman for Dad in the dark days of the early 1980s.

I wasn't so thrilled when I first learned about her. I was at a girlfriend's house in March of 1983 when I got the news.

"Hey, Georgette, your dad is in the paper."

Oh crap, I thought. Most of the big press about "He Stopped Loving Her Today" had died down. Who knew what this was about?

"He got married."

He *what*? I had to learn that my father got married from a *tabloid*?

The minute I saw Mom, I started griping about it. How could my father do this without telling me? Didn't a daughter have the right to know if her father was getting married? Blah, blah. I can still hear me going on and on about it.

Mom did what she always did when the subject of what Dad did came up. She reminded me that he loved me and that he was a good man. That answer didn't cut it, as far as I was concerned. I was mad and nursed the grudge for a couple of years. I guess the day I had to give it up was a couple of years later, when I was fourteen and went to visit Dad and Nancy in Texas. Their house was a long way from the nearest airport, so Dad's two sons picked me up.

Bryan and Jeff were Dad's children with his second wife, Shirley. They were nice guys, and I felt comfortable talking to them. So I told them that I was still upset that I hadn't known about Dad's wedding to Nancy. They looked at each other and burst out laughing.

"Oh yeah?" Bryan said with a laugh. "Well, we didn't know he was married to your mom until we read it in the papers, either!"

I didn't know what to say except "Oh."

They continued to chuckle over my comment, until Bryan added, "Look, that's just Dad. He doesn't tend to things like that. He's not into sending announcements about his doings. Just deal with it."

I decided that I should shut up and deal with it. I wasn't the only person in the world who'd been blindsided by something George Jones had done!

I had met Nancy once before she married Dad. It was on my twelfth birthday, when Dad was in Nashville recording. Since he was at the studio, Nancy took me on a birthday shopping trip, buying me jeans and a pair of cowboy boots. Instead of that endearing her to me, it served to remind me that almost every time I had received presents from Dad it was obvious that someone else had picked them out. They came shipped directly from a store, with a standard gift card. Or worse, they came from his manager or press person, with a note that he had supposedly signed. But it was never in his handwriting.

Still, although I thought that Nancy was okay, I didn't have a clue that they were thinking about getting married. As it turned out, Nancy didn't have a clue, either. He had dropped the news on her with no advance warning.

Dad met Nancy Sepulveda on a blind date, one that he had requested. Dad was in Louisiana with one of his succession of managers in November of 1981. The manager brought along a girlfriend, and Dad offhandedly asked if she had a friend. I don't know whether he was serious about it, and anyway, he was just getting ready to fly to New York for a series of shows. The following day his manager's girlfriend brought Nancy with her to New York.

Dad and Nancy hit it off right away, and I'm sure it was partly because she seemed unimpressed with his star status. I don't mean she didn't love his voice or appreciate his talent, but she didn't come across as celebrity-crazy.

Nancy was a hardworking single mother when she met Dad. And because she couldn't just pick up and run all over the country to see him, Dad often changed his schedule to spend more time with her. He even began booking shows where he would "play for the gate." Given how hot his career was after "He Stopped Loving Her Today," to offer to play a show without a guaranteed payment was astonishing. You have to figure his manager was kicking himself for setting up that blind date in the first place.

They may have fallen in love, but Dad and Nancy are the first to admit that their early years were more wine than roses. (The wine was on Dad's part, not Nancy's.) Nancy had known Dad was a drinker, but she had no idea of the extent to which he imbibed. Nor did she know he was doing cocaine. Her boss at the plant where she was employed, however, seemed to know all about Nancy's new boyfriend. According to Dad, the boss warned Nancy away from the whole relationship because musicians were no good and Dad was the worst of the lot.

Nancy quit her job and went on the road with Dad. Her daughter Adina went with Nancy; the other daughter, Sherry, lived with their father. It was unlike Nancy to do that. She'd had the same job, working on a telephone factory assembly line, for twenty years. She was a responsible person, in no way a party girl or camp follower. So what in the world had possessed her? Well, she saw something in my dad. Maybe it was the same thing my mom had seen, because she, too, followed him. There's another similarity. Like my mom, Nancy hoped she could change Dad.

They had some pretty rough times, and Dad admits he was violent at times. Dad got mixed up with gangster types through his drug use, too, which put him, Nancy, and Adina all at risk. I think that in the end, the knowledge that he'd endangered the lives of people he loved is what started the turnaround.

Nancy worked through it with him, and he did begin to change. Dad says that she never nagged him, but that she stuck with him even when there seemed to be little reason to do so. She fought more with the addiction than she did with Dad. In the end, she won. But she didn't know he was planning on getting married until the day he suddenly blurted out: "We should go get our blood tests."

I wish I could say that I immediately warmed up to Nancy, but I didn't. I caused her all sorts of grief when I was around. I showed little respect and almost no appreciation for anything she did for me.

Even when I tried to fit in, I seemed to mess things up, and then feel inadequate. Sometimes it felt like my dad was testing me. I remember one of the few trips I made to visit him soon after he was married.

"Do you know how to cook, Georgette?" Dad threw out the question almost like an accusation. I thought maybe he was trying to see if Mom had taught me any of his favorite dishes. The trouble was, I didn't know for sure what his favorite dishes were, and God forbid that I'd ask!

"Of course I do," I answered, arrogantly. I didn't really know how to prepare much food, having only watched Mom or one of the cooks, and never with any enthusiasm.

"Well, good. Why don't you fix me something?"

"All right, I will." I'd show him.

There was one thing I thought I could make: chicken and cheese potato casserole. I decided to surprise him, caught a ride to the grocery store, and bought a few things. Then I made the casserole and presented it to him. He didn't eat a bite. It turned out that Dad wasn't a fan of chicken, cheese, or casseroles. He passed on the meal.

Neither of us communicated well *at all*. How simple it would have been for me to ask him if he'd like the casserole, and for him to say no? But that's how we were around each other—mistrusting, easily hurt, and resentful. The worst part of it? I blamed Nancy for the whole debacle because it was easier to point a finger at her than at my father.

FOURTEEN

IN 1983, THE SAME YEAR Dad and Nancy got married, Mom found out that she was going to become a grandmother for the first time. Jackie and her husband, John Paule, had a daughter, Sophia. Mom was delighted with every grandchild, but that first time really thrilled her. She spent hours on the phone telling everyone she knew.

The fact that she was so proud of being a forty-one-year-old grandmother is interesting because this was also a time that her image and age first became an issue. Mom was always insecure—about her voice, her stage show, and her looks.

Mom was heralded as a beauty, but she never felt like she looked good enough. The fact that she didn't have a perfectly straight nose bothered her. (That's a trait I inherited!) Did her hair look just right? And her body, well, she was slim and had a great bustline. You'd think she wouldn't have had any concerns. But she did. For one thing, there was the problem that Mom and Loretta Lynn called Noassitol. *No Ass at All.* They didn't have shapely derrières.

Here's another story Ralph Emery tells:

"One day Tammy called some friends, and said, 'Get over to my house *right now*!'

"Once assembled, she led the group to her bedroom, where her bed was strewn with Frederick's of Hollywood shopping bags. She dipped into one, announcing: 'Girls, I have the answer!' She pulled out a handful of panties with foam rubber padding on the backside.

"Shocked, one stammered, 'Tammy! You want me to wear falsies in my underpants?'

"When her other friends collapsed with laughter, Tammy scolded them. 'I'm serious! We can have real rear ends!'

"Finally, with much urging, the ladies tried on the panties. One friend said, 'Tammy, this is crazy. What will people say when we go from *No-ass-at-all* to *butts you could sit a glass of water on*?'"

MOM WAS CAPABLE of joking about her rear, or her nose, but she was easily hurt by criticism. One of the many traits I had grown to dislike in Richey was his habit of putting down Mom about how she looked. He knew how sensitive she was, yet he continued to point out real and imagined flaws. The tendency to sneer extended to my sisters and me, as well, although he usually made his comments to us when Mom was not present. Sometimes he made ugly remarks about how we looked, and at other times, about our level of intelligence. All of us tried to ignore the slights, but it wasn't always easy. Dealing with criticism was especially difficult for someone as sensitive as Mom was.

Because she was so easily intimidated about her looks, Mom loved people who just blew off those concerns. John Anderson is a case in point. Mom loved his music and respected the way he approached his career. They first met on Mom's bus in the early 1980s, when John was opening a show for her. She said he was one of the most humble, laid-back, normal guys in the business. She liked the fact that he seemed a little quiet and shy. Sitting there on the bus, John confessed to her that his label had tried to get him to make some changes about his appearance when he first signed his contract. They wanted him to have a stylist of their choice redo his whole image. They wanted a shorter haircut, cooler clothes—and they wanted him to get his teeth straightened. John told them no. He explained that if they wanted his music, they could take him just like he was. He told Mom that his conversation went like this:

"I'm not fixin' to do any of that stuff. If you want me, you take me, long hair and crooked teeth. I might comb my hair a little more careful and get a new jeans jacket. Minor things. But if you don't think I look good enough, if you think I'm too much of a hillbilly, then don't sign me. I'm gonna make the music I want and look the way I feel comfortable looking. Anything else wouldn't be me."

Mom said she never forgot that, because some people were the opposite, the kind that would probably think it over if their label asked them to get a sex change! Mom never liked seeing the business change to where image was more important than the music. Don't get me wrong: she understood looking good and projecting an image. But she wished that it was allowed to come naturally, and from the artists themselves.

Still, Mom was nervous about age, and it really bothered her when people referred to it. Once, when she heard a young singer suggest that she and other older artists should get out of the way for the younger ones, she famously said, "Move me." She was only in her late thirties or early forties when that was said! And she really did stay mad about it. She told me she didn't care if she ever worked with that young woman again. In her world, artists stood together. You were supportive and didn't trash-talk each other.

But when Epic Records suggested an image update, Mom was happy to comply. For one thing, she knew the label was right. She needed to move into the '80s. For another, the man working the closest with her was the VP of marketing, Mike Martinovich. Mom loved Mike, and he loved her. She knew that he would never suggest anything unless he believed it was in her best interest, and I believe she was right. And so she had wardrobe consultants, stage show choreographers, photographers, and hairstylists. Mom got a new, updated, short hairstyle and a simple yet classy wardrobe.

The new Tammy was introduced on *Sometimes When We Touch*, produced by Steve Buckingham. Richey had produced several albums for Mom, and when they went nowhere, Buckingham was brought in. She also had a new manager, Stan Moress. Neither Moress nor Buckingham lasted long under the Richey regime, but they were around long enough for the image transformation.

Not long after the release of *Sometimes When We Touch,* Mom opened up about her age concerns with a journalist that she knew. She was rehearsing at Sound Stage in Nashville, and when the writer showed up, Mom had just sat down in the room where the musicians were setting up. But one of the first things this writer mentioned was how great Mom's new hairdo looked. At that point, Mom seemed to get a little apprehensive, and she asked the woman to come to another place to do the interview.

When they got to a little room in the back, Mom got out her cigarettes and confessed that she was supposed to be trying to quit and wanted to smoke in private. She also said she wanted to talk off the record. She said she was worried about getting older in a young business and that she was sometimes scared. She *hated* being afraid. They talked about how unfair it was that the male artists got a pass on wrinkles, while the women were held to a different standard. The writer told her about a funny comment Lacy J. Dalton once said: "Women will be equal in this business when we can have as many wrinkles as Willie, and nobody says anything."

Mom knew all that, of course. She knew that time passed and that there was little you could do about it. She knew that other women felt the same pressure. But knowing didn't make it any easier.

FIFTEEN

THROUGHOUT 1983, MOM AND RICHEY had been dropping hints about moving to Florida. Mom loved living near water, loved having a beach in close proximity. Old Hickory Lake, where she had so often taken refuge, wasn't quite the same—Mom wanted ocean air.

I hated the idea of moving back to Florida and told Mom so. I knew too well what a transition this meant: new address, new school, new kids. I'd been there before. If I changed schools again, it would make eight schools I'd attended. That includes a few where Mom enrolled me only to decide she didn't like something about the place and pull me out almost immediately. I was sick of being the new kid, of having to figure out the new building, the teachers, and the cliques. I just wanted to stay at Harding

Academy, where I had some good friends and was doing okay in my classes.

Mom listened and considered what I'd said. They were moving no matter what, and Mom knew it. But she wanted me to be at least satisfied with the plan.

"I promise that you will be able to stay in the school you want until you graduate high school," she explained. "This will be the end of jumping from school to school."

"Are you sure?"

"Yes," she said firmly.

And so we moved. For a short time, it looked like we were going to be one big happy family again. Gwen and Jackie were both married by then, and Mom asked them to come to Florida with their families. Things got dicey almost immediately.

One of the reasons Mom had asked Gwen to move back was so that she could help her try and sort through some new companies that were being set up, businesses she didn't know about and hadn't authorized. This next part is hard to tell, because I believe that it represents a low point in Mom's life.

Mom became convinced that Richey was hiding some kind of papers from her—important documents—and that he kept them in his locked briefcase. She enlisted Gwen and Jackie, their husbands, and even Tina in a plan whereby she would get Richey out of the house, and they would try to break into the briefcase. The plan went horribly wrong when Mom chickened out and confessed everything to Richey. He went into a rage and threw everyone out, even teenage Tina. She went back to Nashville and lived with her friend Lisa McPherson and her mom. I guess I was too young to have been allowed in on the plan, or I might have been kicked out, too.

Forever after, that episode would be known to Mom's daughters as "the briefcase affair."

I don't know what Mom was thinking. My best guess is that she knew that she was being cut out of her own business just as surely as she'd been taken out of the child support payment loop. I'm surprised that she even brought it up to Gwen and Jackie. Mom was very discreet about her business. If she did know what decisions were being made, she usually kept the information to herself. But in this case, something was going on to cause her to question Richey's expertise, if not his honesty. In fear, she turned to the ones she knew she could trust: her daughters.

The trouble is, she didn't have much strength when it came to Richey. Even when it came to what amounted to an injustice done to her children, she caved. I lay that squarely at the door of pain and medication.

It caused a rift in the family that lasted for a long time. Gwen and Jackie didn't feel like they could trust her, and rightfully so. I think by then she was scared to let Richey go his own way with her business, yet even more fearful of finding out something that would force her to make the decision to leave.

NOT WANTING TO take a chance on me finding another class-cutting crowd, Mom enrolled me in Jupiter Christian School. That was fine with me but for one detail: the school had a dress code. I was still very much a tomboy at age fourteen, and I disliked wearing dresses. *Dislike* is too tame a word; it was more like I hated wearing them. Jeans were my style.

I hated fixing my hair, too. I even threw away the notices about picture day once when I was in grade school, knowing that Mom would want me to curl my hair and wear a dress. One time I showed up wearing my hair in pigtails and a T-shirt that had the following words sandwiched in between a graphic of two buns: "Two all-beef patties special sauce lettuce cheese pickles onions on a sesame seed bun." Unfortunately, Mom took one look at the photo, called the school to find out when the photo makeup day was, then made sure that I was there and dressed properly. Hair curled and all.

Mom and I had argued about my clothing choices for several years before we moved back to Florida. When she was on the road, she'd buy me piles of very feminine clothes: dresses, skirts, blouses. She'd go back out on the road, and when she returned, she'd go through my closet and find them all hanging with the tags still attached. Finally, Mom had an idea. She'd require us to get dressed up and go to church every Sunday. From that day on, our nanny insisted we follow Mom's instructions.

We were raised Christians, but because Mom was usually driving back from a show on Sundays, we hadn't often gone to church. Under her new plan, it didn't matter if she was home or not. Unless we were with her on that tour bus, we were supposed to be cleaned up and sitting in church on Sunday.

Tina had an answer for Mom's strategy. Once she got her driver's license, Tina pretended to take us to church, fooling the nanny in charge. We'd get dressed up, drive to our church, and pick up a program, then head to one of her friend's houses and change into our jeans and T-shirts. Even if someone asked us about the service, we could wing it. All it took was reading through the programs we'd lifted.

I made up for those lost Sundays at Jupiter Christian, because we had to attend Bible classes every day. I do feel that I became much more spiritual while I was at the school. That was probably due to some of the time I spent alone, studying Bible lessons. What I did more than "study" was to sit and reflect on the world and what those teachings meant. I think that I got more out of that than if I'd been memorizing verses.

I wasn't a great student at Jupiter Christian, just average, really. I listened to the teachers and did my homework without ever putting in any extra effort. Mom insisted I make at least a C, and was pleased that I made mostly A's and B's with just an occasional C in math or science.

Not surprisingly, I was in the school choir and played in the band. My first choices were the saxophone or the flute, but the band already had too many of both instruments, so I ended up playing the French horn for about a year.

My favorite classes were English and history. I loved to read, write, and put myself in other times and places through the history books. I think that traveling with Mom when she was touring in Europe made a big difference in the way I felt about those history classes. In that way, Mom had been right a year earlier when she told my school that my two weeks in Europe would be an important educational experience. It was. I think it changed the way I saw other countries and cultures, making me forever curious.

I loved writing short stories and poetry. Even though I didn't see either of those exercises as a prelude to songwriting, both were. I started seeing structure and rhyme and how both could work together to tell a story in song. I'm glad I came to songwriting this way, rather than just assuming that because both of my parents wrote songs, that I should somehow "get it" by osmosis.

I liked the biological sciences, but not physics or chemistry. That I disliked math but enjoyed geometry was due to one of the geometry teachers. She made the subject easy and interesting. She also was a very casual woman who wore skirts, but with sneakers or loafers, very informal. I think I realized for the first time how important having even one inspiring teacher can be.

EVEN THOUGH I wasn't what I consider a serious student for most of my high school years, I think I understood basic study skills and could implement them when needed. That would prove an invaluable ability in just a couple of years when I doubled up on my eleventh- and twelfth-grade studies. I credit my grandparents for that capability. MeeMaw, the former teacher, always encouraged me along academic lines. And when I was younger and staying with them, PeePaw was quick to sit down with me to work on my studies. Mom was actively involved when she wasn't on the road. When she was gone, I counted on Cathye Leshay.

I dated a lot in high school, and—with the exception of one period—was popular at Jupiter Christian. Despite being a new kid, I was elected cheerleader every year and

Carolyn, Flora and Chester Russell (my great-grandparents), and Mom, taken by Meemaw around 1948.

Jackie, Gwen, and Tina, taken by Meemaw, I'm guessing 1968 or 1969.

Granma Jones, Mom, and Daddy, taken by Meemaw around 1969.

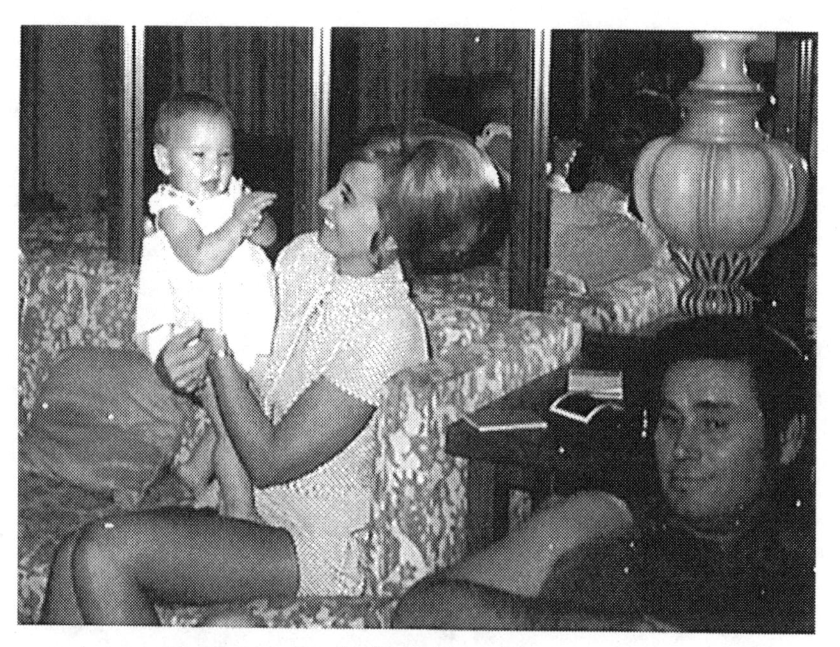

Me, Mom, and Dad at home, taken by Meemaw, 1971.

Me and Mom, taken by Meemaw, 1971.

Tina, Jackie, Daddy, me, Mom, and an unknown girl,
taken on my birthday in 1971 by Meemaw.

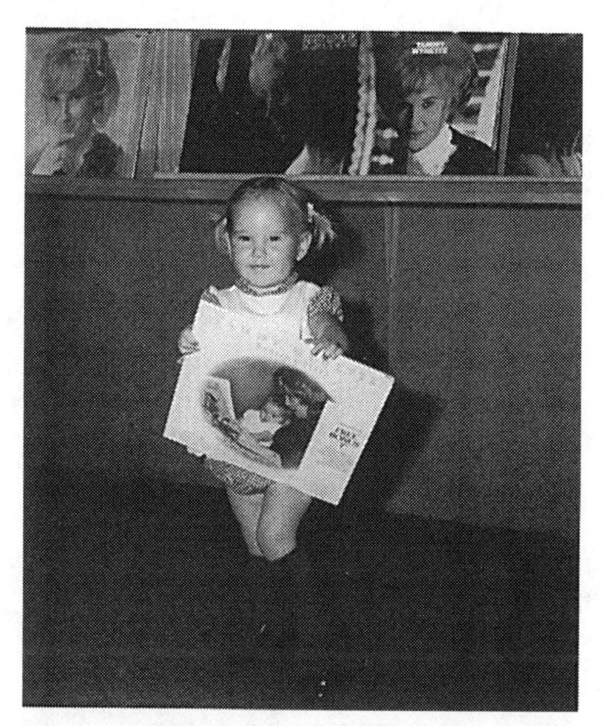

Me at the Music Park gift shop, taken by Meemaw in 1972.

Me and Mom, 1976.

Mom and Dad onstage, 1972.

Daddy, me, and Mom at a *Hee Haw* show, I'm guessing 1977.

Me and Kriston Jetton, taken by Meemaw in 1978.

Taken by Meemaw in Ireland in 1982: me, Mom, and Tina.

Naomi Judd, Mom, Wynonna Judd, Loretta Lynn, and Ashley Judd, around 1990.

Bryan White, Stonewall Jackson, Crystal Gayle, Milton Berle, Mom, Holly Dunn, and Ray Stevens, around 1990.

Dad onstage in the early 1990s.

Me, Mom, and our friend Lisa at my college graduation, December 1992, taken by Joel Smith.

Daddy holding Kyle, and me holding Ryan, taken by Nancy at their home in 1994.

Mom and Dad, around 1995.

Mom and Dad on a talk show, 1995.

Dad and Nancy, around 1998.

Ryan, Grandma, and Kyle, taken by me in May 2005 on the tour bus.

Me and Nancy, taken by Nancy's daughter, Sherry Hohimer, in 2006.

Me at my RCA showcase in 2007, taken by Scotty Kennedy.

Me and Jamie backstage in Belfast, Ireland, in August 2009, taken by our friend Erin Hardiman.

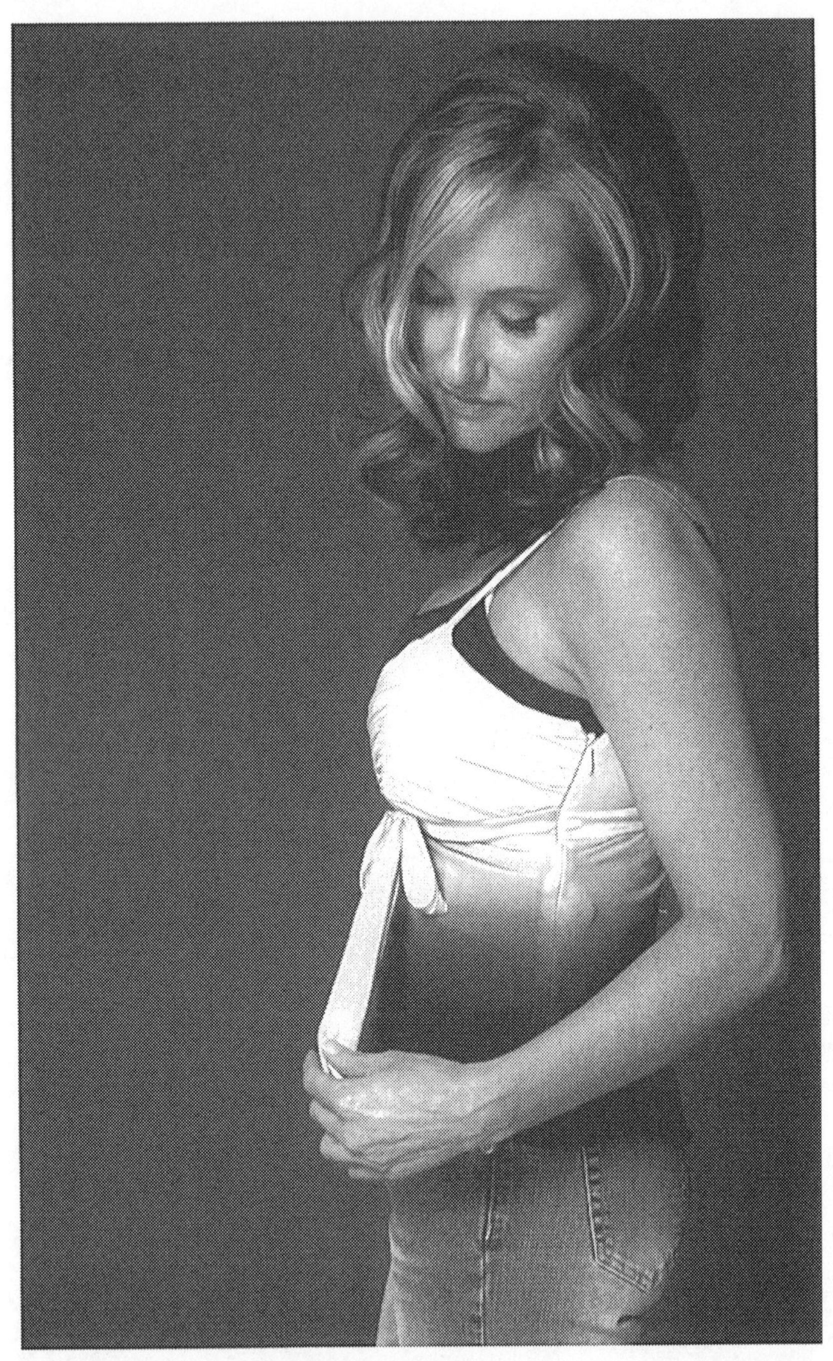

A photo of me taken in 2006 by Rusty Russell for the cover of *A Slightly Used Woman*.
This album was released in March 2010 by Heart of Texas Records.

was always in the Homecoming Court. It was such a big deal at our house when I was first elected to the court during my eighth-grade year. Mom was so excited you'd have thought I'd won a Grammy! She even drove the convertible in the homecoming parade, with my escort and me sitting in the back waving to the crowds along the street.

Between high school classes and extracurricular activities, going on the road with Mom became more difficult. I'd loved every minute of being out there with her. If not for those experiences, the years between my childhood and my late teens would have been so much different. On the road was where I really got to know my mother. That's where I saw, for example, just how adventuresome she was—just how quickly she wanted to show people the side of her that had sunk the hook shot for Richey's nephews. It's possible that she was reminding herself that she wasn't losing herself in her last marriage.

One thing she loved to do was drive the tour bus. I've known very few women who wanted to drive the bus! But Mom did. And she was a good driver. When she was touring with Ronnie Milsap, she mentioned her bus-driving prowess to some of the guys in Ronnie's band while they were packing up to leave a venue.

"No way a girl drives that bus," one of them said.

"We'll see about that," she said, with a self-assured smile.

The buses took off, and several miles down the road, the Tammy Wynette bus—with Mom driving—pulled past the Ronnie Milsap bus. She honked and waved. But Ronnie's crew was not to be outdone. Five minutes later, their bus passed Mom—with Ronnie at the wheel! (It goes without saying that they faked that scene, with Ronnie sitting right up next to the window and the driver scrunched down beside him.)

Those great times, and the closeness I felt when we shared time talking or shopping or singing together, were vital to our relationship. When we were together off the road, there was always something going on. There were so many people demanding her time, so much activity. But on that bus, and in strange cities together, it was us.

As much as I loved being out there on the road with her, I cut back on the tours after I was about fourteen. I was beginning to find myself in high school.

Once I got to Jupiter Christian, I discovered something about myself. I had been a lonely child, even though I was never really alone. In fact, there was usually a lot going on around me: people and activity everywhere. But my sisters were older and into their own goings-on. Mom tried to make time for us, and in so many ways was one of the most exciting parents you could imagine. But I yearned for intimacy. The many times I hid in those secret rooms in various houses might have been a clue to how I felt; I needed a smaller, more personal world. I needed a world with close friends, and instead, I seemed to have playmates. I didn't go spend a weekend or an overnight with a girlfriend. Nor did they spend nights with me. Instead, I had playdates.

It would be easy to say that Mom's entertainer status was the key factor, but I don't think it was. There were times that I was teased about both parents' celebrity, times when people made assumptions about me because of their larger-than-life personas. For one thing, and this has lasted to this day, many assumed that I was rich. I had access to a wealthy lifestyle when I lived at home, but that is far different from being rich yourself.

Events can play out similarly in any big, active family where the parents are pulled in many directions and one child has some trouble trying to establish an identity. I made friends, and I found myself wanting to spend more time with them while I was in school in Jupiter, Florida. It was there that I finally developed my individuality.

The one difficult time I had during high school occurred in the ninth grade, when I found that I was getting a reputation as being "easy." It was a ridiculous accusation. I was a virgin, and although I dated regularly, I didn't "date around." I had one boyfriend at a time and didn't have sex with any of them.

The problem, and many of you women will understand it, was my breast size. Like my mother, I had very large breasts—great at twenty-four, not so much at fourteen. If I could have done it, I would have opted for a breast reduction at that young age. For a while, I was treated badly by the girls, while most of the boys were asking for my phone number. There were more than a few taunts hurled my way in the halls, too.

The slutty girl reputation is a tricky thing to combat. It took me holding my head high and working very hard to keep my self-esteem up to make it through. Mom would have been fired up had she known what I was going through. But I never said a word. It was far too embarrassing.

Eventually the talk subsided, and I was put back in the "nice girl" side of the equation. The time when I was most considered a "good girl" was when I was sixteen and dating a boy who planned on being a youth pastor. We went to church every Sunday and Bible study on Wednesday nights. If anything at all was going on at the church, we were in the thick of it. And that, as you probably can guess, was the boy with whom I first had sex.

Oh, the irony.

SIXTEEN

CHURCH WAS IMPORTANT TO ME. I attended Mom's Baptist church on Sundays if she was home and the Maranatha Church, in West Palm Beach, the rest of the time. Maranatha was Pentecostal, so I ended up calling myself a "Bapticostal."

I've never attended church anywhere that had better playing and singing than Maranatha. They had a full band, with concerts featuring everything from old-time gospel to modern Christian music. I especially liked Amy Grant and Petra, and played their records nonstop.

And it was through the Maranatha Church that I set out on a life-changing trip in 1986. We went on a mission to Haiti for ten days, working with medical teams in several different villages. We'd been briefed and trained, but nothing can prepare you for seeing such poverty and despair for the first time.

Haiti was in troubled times during 1986. The streets were filled with protests against President Jean-Claude Duvalier, "Baby Doc," as they called him. We were warned against complaining about the officials that would search our bags on arrival, told that they might take items they wanted from our belongings. This was long before 9/11, and Americans had seldom seen tight controls at airports. We were lucky to be treated well when we arrived at the Port-au-Prince airport, and that caused us to let our guard down.

As far as we knew, food and water was our biggest danger. We brought our own food, each of us packing one of our suitcases with nothing but canned goods we planned to eat. We were instructed not only to drink only bottled water, but also never to even brush our teeth with anything else.

Our first stop in Port-au-Prince was the Missionary Home, where we received more information about the village hospitals. On the following day, we went on a tour of the city, and what we saw was stunning. In addition to the obvious destitution throughout Port-au-Prince, there was an all-encompassing air of danger; you knew that the whole city could explode in violence at any time. This seemed at odds with the friendly manner in which we'd been received at the airport.

On the second morning, along with a team of translators, we headed for the jungle in a tap-tap truck, with a long extended bed and benches down each side. The bed and sides were covered in colorful tin cans that had been welded together into a canopy to keep people dry in case of a sudden thunderstorm. We drove for twelve hours before coming to the first village, where the extent of the people's plight was right in our faces. They had *nothing*. The soil was no longer good for growing, and they had fished until only the smallest of catches remained. There was no sanitation, and the water was contaminated. There wasn't even a way to warm food, so we ate the foods we brought cold from the cans.

We quickly got into the routine we would follow at each village for the next week. We set up our medical mini-clinics outdoors. The villagers took numbers and then started through the process in an orderly manner. First, they saw a nurse to explain if they had a specific problem to address and have their vital signs taken. Next, they met with a doctor who would determine what health problems they faced and what treatment they needed. Finally, they came to us, the volunteers. We were taught to give them shots if needed and to take them to the pharmacy section for whatever meds had been prescribed. It was at that first village that I began to develop an interest in medicine as a possible profession.

This was no summer camp for American church kids. During the time we were in Haiti, we slept outside on the ground, rain or shine. We had only bamboo mats, not even sleeping bags or pillows. It was over a hundred degrees every day, and we had no showers. You can imagine that within a day or so we were pretty foul.

Then one night it rained. We awakened in cranky moods, with those drops of water falling faster and faster on our faces. But what a godsend it was! We grabbed our bottles of antibacterial soap and started washing. We were fully clothed, scrubbing our bodies and "doing our laundry" all at the same time. We also collected rainwater in buckets to try to stay clean the next day. By the time the rain ended, everyone was laughing and dancing, realizing that when you have so little, joy can be found in the simplest things.

In the short time we were there, I came to love the people of Haiti. I learned a bit of the language, which was a sort of blending of French and Creole. It meant a lot to be able to communicate somewhat, and on their terms. We sang together and played games with the children. These were a wonderful and kind people, but poverty-stricken and unhealthy. The hardest part was in knowing that we could only do so much. We couldn't solve all their problems.

One of the most pressing issues with many of the people in the villages was the status of their children. About a year earlier, many children had been taken back to the city to the missionary house. They had such horrific illnesses that there was no way to treat them in their village. All the parents we met with had willingly sent their children because they were terrified that they were dying, but lines of communication were poor, and they often had no news for months at a time. I thought what courage and desperation it took for these villagers to turn their children over to strangers. But the death rate of children was so high—many died before they turned five years of age—that the parents were literally shoving them into the arms of medical workers heading back to the missionary home.

I'd met some of those children when we first arrived in Port-au-Prince, and my heart was broken over one little girl in particular. Her name was Rosella. She was around two years old when she'd come to the home. In her case, no one awaited news. Rosella's mother had died in childbirth, and her father died not long after she came to Port-au-Prince for treatment for malnutrition. Even when she was in much better shape, no one would claim her. And so Rosella would live at the home until she was old enough to live on her own. It was certainly better than dying in the jungle, but it left her terribly alone.

I left Haiti a changed person. For the first time in my life I realized what a blessing it was to know that I would always have food and clothing. One way or another, I would always have a roof over my head. And even in trying times, I would always have hope. These were a people with almost *no* hope. Events in Haiti in 2009 took me back to those little villages and to those people. You have to wonder how much individuals can go through and why some seem to be destined to take pounding after pounding.

When we packed up to leave, we were unprepared for what had transpired in Port-au-Prince. Given the relative ease with which we'd entered the country, we had no fears about getting out. But the unrest we'd felt in the city streets had been more urgent than any of us suspected. After a five-hour boat ride back to the town where we were to meet the tap-tap, we found that no truck had arrived and no word as to why. The town did have one telephone, so a call was made to the mission home. When we finally got through, the news was alarming.

Baby Doc Duvalier had been deposed by a military coup, and a two-day strike was declared. No one in the entire country was allowed to work or even to drive. We slept that night on the floor of the town's church, while the local missionaries rounded up three jeeps to get us back to the city. The drive was more difficult than it would have been in the tap-tap truck, because we had to cross water from time to time. But we eventually made it to Port-au-Prince. Once there we faced angry crowds because we were driving during the strike. People shouted threats and pelted the jeeps with rocks all through the city to the mission home.

We arrived two days later than planned, so there wasn't even time to take a shower. Believe me, we needed showers! But we scrambled onto our plane, sweaty and stinking, just in the nick of time to get out of the country safely. My mom was beside herself with worry, unable to learn what was happening until I landed in the United States and could call her. I'm sure that Mom would have fought me over it, but I would have gone back once the immediate danger had passed.

Seventeen

AT HOME, RICHEY WAS PUSHING Mom to move back to Nashville. This wasn't a complete surprise. I knew that something was going wrong with their businesses even though Mom almost never shared any information about it. I'd hear about some shopping mall or other opportunity, but never enough to know what was going on. For me, all it meant was that it seemed to be connected with a desire to leave Florida.

Mom kept telling Richey that she'd given me her word. She insisted that she must allow me to finish high school. But I knew how Richey worked her, and it worried me. I was determined to graduate from high school in Florida.

The biggest red flag was when Mom and Richey moved from the house in Jupiter Inlet Colony into a condo in Tequesta, just down the road. I could feel time running out on me. So, as a high school junior, I decided to finish all my credits for graduation in one year. I was proven right when Mom and Richey bought another house in Nashville. They started spending more time there, leaving Cathye and me in the condo.

Mom was very supportive of me finishing early if I was sure that's what I wanted to do. She knew that it meant giving up being in the Homecoming Court and many other senior year extracurricular activities. But I know she wanted to help me stay at Jupiter, no matter what. For a long time, I wasn't sure what Richey thought about any of it—my finishing early, my college plans—anything having to do with school.

Then one day I heard him talking on the telephone in the office. I've never known for sure to whom he was speaking, but I suspected it was one of his family members. My name was mentioned, so I listened.

"Georgette may finish high school early, but I doubt it. Even if she does, she'll never go to college. She'll probably just get married and pop out a few kids. That's all she'll do."

The hair stood up on the back of my neck. I didn't think he'd talk that way about me. It brought out the Jones in me. I went underground with my books and finished the classwork, graduating in 1987. By then, Mom and Richey were living in Nashville nearly full-time.

Richey ended up convincing Mom that I couldn't get the work completed, and that I wouldn't graduate. I know why he did it. They desperately needed the money. They'd had to file for bankruptcy over a couple of shopping mall investments gone bad, and the only way they could start to dig out was if Mom took every booking possible. That meant she had to keep working no matter how bad she felt, no matter how much pain medication it took—and no matter if it meant booking a date on the very night I was supposed to graduate from high school.

I know she resisted, but as usual, in the end Richey won. Mom was on the road when I graduated. MeeMaw and PeePaw came from Alabama to see me get my diploma.

There is a heroine in this story. I took my twelfth-grade classes from the University of Pensacola Christian School, with the help of a woman named Susie Stonecipher. She was the mother of my friend Misi Stonecipher and taught at Jupiter Christian. It was only because of Susie that I could make my plan work. She set it up where she could tutor me if needed, monitor my tests, and supervise the program. For that, I will forever be grateful.

THERE WAS ANOTHER debate about my schooling that year. This time it involved college "discussions" between my mom and my dad. I was still dating the boy who wanted to be a youth pastor, the first boy I had ever had sex with. We planned on going to college together, and at his urging, we visited Oral Roberts University in Tulsa, Oklahoma. It seemed like a wonderful campus, with a good Christian environment and a solid curriculum. We decided to enroll.

Everything was set for our return that fall—or it was until Mom called and told Dad. As it turned out, Dad had seen a recent news story about Oral Roberts telling his television audience that unless he raised a million dollars "God would call him home."

Dad was disgusted at what he considered an underhanded attempt to get contributions from the very people who could probably least afford to be giving money: sick people, shut-ins, retirees—people on small, fixed incomes. He was dead set against me going to Oral Roberts University. Mom told me what he'd said, but she told me that the choice was mine. At first, I went ahead with my boyfriend's plan to attend ORU.

I wasn't happy with my decision, though. I understood Dad's reservations and agreed that Pastor Roberts was essentially blackmailing his followers. Plus, I very much wanted to do something that pleased Dad. And so, just two weeks before I was ready to head to Tulsa, I told my boyfriend that I had changed my mind about going with him. We had a long talk about it and decided that since we would be at different schools, we should break up. Both of us knew that the long-distance relationship wouldn't work.

I enrolled at the University of North Alabama and got an apartment in Florence. Mom hauled some furniture and kitchenware from storage in Nashville and then bought me some additional chairs for the living room. We went to a Walmart in Florence and got a few things like bedding, towels, silverware. Mom chose some pictures to hang on the wall. She loved having a little decorating project, reminding me every so often of how good my dad was at design. Mom seldom missed an opportunity to praise my dad even during times I know she might have been angry with him.

What a fun time that was—having Mom all to myself for shopping, talking, planning. She was in great shape, healthy and seemingly drug free.

I was excited and nervous at the same time. Moving

into my own little place at the Polynesian Village complex seemed like the best thing in the world. But my nervousness proved to be a warning, because it turned out to be one of the worst. I was in no way prepared to be in charge of my own life. For one thing, I had no idea what it cost to live! I had barely seen an electric bill or known just what everyday supplies cost. I don't know where I thought toilet paper, bath soap, shampoo, and toothpaste came from, but I soon learned they were all items you have to buy at a store every so often!

Mom sent me an allowance every month, but it never lasted. I'd be calling back home to the office, asking if I could get an advance on the next month. And if I visited Mom or went to see MeeMaw and PeePaw, I always took a box of supplies back with me. I'm sure plenty of college students know that scam—shopping in Mom's pantry.

It's also easy for college students who live in dorms or sorority houses to assume that anyone living in an apartment is up for swinging parties at any given moment. It's very hard for a sixteen-year-old to know how to respond to older teens or students in their early twenties. You just don't have the life experience to deal with it. I was always afraid that I would make someone mad or offend in some way.

Another problem, and one that became part of a larger issue, was my fear of living alone. I didn't know I had that fear, not really. I didn't know what it would feel like to go to bed and know that no one was anywhere near. I was the one who always tried to scoot into my parents' bed as a small child. I liked having my sisters and nannies around. I didn't like hearing a board creak in the night and hoping it was just the building settling. Those fears made it very easy to start doing the same thing I had seen my mother do time and again: insist on having a man to rely on at all times. And if I ever needed proof of how that reliance could go wrong, it happened once again in regards to Richey.

During my first year of college, Richey called me and asked me to come home and participate in a drug intervention with Mom. In spite of the fact that she was fine much of the time I was around her—times like the move into my apartment in Florence—I knew that she was taking too much pain medication. I knew she needed to do something about it.

"She's gotta quit taking drugs," Richey said. "I need your help."

"Of course I'll come," I said. I wanted so much to believe that he was serious that I jumped at the chance to help.

My sisters and I all came, arriving while Mom and Richey were out on the road. But from the minute I walked into the house, something seemed fishy. There was a preacher and a drug counselor there. So I wondered why, if this was such an emergency, Richey's own children were not there. He always made such an issue out of the fact that we were one big happy family. Unfortunately, I didn't think hard enough about that missing piece of the equation.

"What are you doing here?" Mom exclaimed when she walked in. She seemed at once thrilled and suspicious.

And so it began. We started telling her how we were concerned about her, that we loved her and wanted her to be well. Mom looked thunderstruck, and I looked to Richey for some kind of backup. But there was no backup coming from him.

"I can't believe you girls would do this," he said coldly. "How could you confront her when she's been out working hard and comes to her own home exhausted?"

Our jaws must have looked like they were ready to hit the floor.

"I won't be a part of this!" Richey said, and then stormed out of the room leaving the four of us standing there in front of Mom—trapped rats.

"I can't believe it, either," Mom said, turning to me. "You, Georgette! You've never done something like this to your father! Why are you doing it to me?"

I don't know where I got the courage to say it, but I answered honestly. "I don't have a real relationship with my father. If I did, I would do this very thing. But I do have a relationship with you, Mom. And I want you alive and healthy."

We got through that disaster, and just as my sisters had put "the briefcase affair" behind them, we all moved on for the time being. I returned to college, and we spoke no more about it.

Too often, too much was left unsaid.

Eighteen

MY FIRST SEMESTER AT UNA was filled with the usual freshman classes: English literature, American history, earth science. I still loved reading and literature, and for a time considered going for a teaching degree. Then, in my second semester, I took a photography class and fell in love with the whole experience. I loved both taking the photos and the process involved in developing them. I could easily see myself pursuing a career in photography. And in the back of my mind was the newly acquired passion I'd felt working with the doctors and nurses among those Haitian villagers.

Music remained the elephant in the room.

I loved singing backup for Mom, the feeling of being a part of her world, the screaming crowds. But I knew what that applause was about. I understood that people wanted to see Tammy Wynette and George Jones's daughter up there singing, and I never once mistook my talent for that of my parents. Standing on the stage with Mom was fun but incredibly intimidating. Her voice was magic, and no matter how many people told me that I could sing, I always knew I was not in the same class. As time went by, I felt expectations rising about what I might do. Was I going to try to be a star? Could I cut it on my own? As it turned out, I didn't take that chance. The reason had less to do with any real or perceived talent, but more to do with my insecurities. It was easy to stand in Mom's shadow, not so easy when it came to stepping out alone.

Mom's attitudes about stardom had an effect on me, as well. It's true that she kept her beautician's license current, or at least she renewed it most years. She saw people get eaten alive by the music business, and she saw fame as fragile. There was always that question in my mind: if Tammy Wynette can't trust this kind of a career, what chance did I have? Security was very important to me.

I had one experience as an older teen that led me to believe I might go for a future in music. Peggy Lynn, Cindy Cash, and Kathy Twitty approached me with an offer to join a group they were starting. Called the Next Generation, they had some early interest from RCA and a group promoting Canadian concerts. We rehearsed, started putting together a show, and got excited about our prospects. But we never could work out one glaring problem: I was the only one who could sing harmony. I didn't see that we could call ourselves a group if we just sang one song together, and I was the only one who sang harmony on it. You could have added some harmony singers, but with four already in the group, I didn't think it could work.

In the end, my decision to attend college and aim for a "day job" had to do with my longings for a real family life. By the time I finished high school, Dad was seldom around. He'd become almost a nonentity unless I read about him in the newspapers. For that reason, I wanted to be married, to have children—lots of children. I wanted to find a husband who would be a full-time father. And I wanted to raise children in a normal, stable setting. Despite all the benefits of traveling with Mom and the allure of the spotlight, my need for a real home life became the driving factor in my choices.

I IMMEDIATELY STARTED dating a lot, because I hated being by myself. Surprisingly, in that new situation, the one I married was a boy I'd known for years!

He was the first boy I ever held hands with, which happened at a drive-in movie when I was twelve and visiting MeeMaw and PeePaw in Red Bay, Alabama. No kissing. No making out in the car. We just held hands. The funny part of it is that we didn't date after that until I was in my late teens, in college in Alabama. I was back in Red Bay and saw him at a party. We talked and laughed over our first little "date" so long ago. He was funny, nice, and respectful.

His name was Billy Terrell, and he was everything I thought I wanted.

Our relationship developed quickly. Billy moved into my apartment with me, and proposed in July of 1988. Because Billy and I were already living together, and I was my mother's daughter, I thought that I should be married.

BILLY WAS AN outgoing guy who never knew a stranger, the life of every party. He was a bull rider who raced cars and seemed to be having a good time every minute of the day. He was the guy who won every drinking contest and told the funniest jokes. He kept everyone laughing. I thought we'd get married and have this great big fun life ahead of us. We set a wedding date of March 5, 1989. Mom was not thrilled about it.

"Why don't you just get engaged?" she asked. "You can finish college and then plan the wedding."

"But I love him!"

"If you love him now, you'll love him just as much when you finish the four years of college," she said.

I wouldn't listen, and she didn't push it.

I decided that this wedding was going to be worthy of a fairy tale, and I called my dad to tell him the date. He would walk me down the aisle and give me away. Or so I thought. What I didn't expect was this conversation:

"Daddy, guess what? Billy and I are getting married! I'm so in love! I want you to walk me down the aisle."

There was a long silence over the phone line, then finally, Dad spoke.

"Georgette, just because he asked you to marry him doesn't mean you have to do it."

I wouldn't listen to him, just as I didn't listen to Mom.

I was in love and getting married. We were holding it in Red Bay, Alabama, on March 5, and I wanted my father to be there.

There was another long silence.

"I'm working on the fourth. I'll probably be too tired to do it."

That was it. He would talk no more of it. And I was shattered. I could not believe that my dad would blow off my wedding with the excuse of anticipated fatigue. It would take me years to understand his reactions, how guarded he is, and how hard it is for him to have the fatherly talks I so wanted. Of course, I didn't show him in any way that I was open to having a talk. I just ignored his concern and breezed right along with my plan. And so he shut down.

I reacted in a childish manner. I sent out invitations that read: Mr. and Mrs. George Richey invite you to the wedding of Georgette Jones and Billy Terrell. Then, since PeePaw had recently died, I asked Richey to walk me down the aisle.

I don't know if Dad would have come to the wedding and given me away or not. I do know that he was hurt at the snub. I was hurt, he was hurt. And nobody talked to each other about it. As I look back on times like that, I want to rewrite the script. I want us to sit down and go over the "whys and wherefores" of the incident. I was genuinely hurt by his actions, as was he by mine. But in those days, conversations and honesty seemed impossible.

Billy and I decided to attend Mississippi State the following year. PeePaw had passed away in '88, and MeeMaw's health was failing. Before she finally moved into Mom's house, she moved closer to some of her relatives in Alabama. So Billy and I moved into her house in Red Bay for a summer. Then we moved to Auburn, Alabama, where Billy could attend pharmacy school and I could get a nursing degree.

IT WAS WHILE I was in college and a newlywed that I realized that I had to be on guard continually—not against others, but against myself.

Billy was the life of the party. Everyone loved being around him. And back in those days, he never turned down a good time. I found myself sliding into the party life right along with him.

My marriage to Billy didn't last long. I learned that he hadn't been going to most of his pharmacy classes. I guess his partying took away any ambition he'd had. I had been trying to keep up with him, partying while working in the emergency room and going to classes. It all unraveled when I suspected he was cheating on me. By that time, I'd met another man.

Yes, yes—I know. There's that tendency to jump from one man to another.

Billy and I separated in November of 1990. Then I filed for divorce and moved on. Mom and Dad had both been right—I should have waited to marry in the first place. But I believe that the lesson I learned was vital. I slowly began to be aware of the fact that I had a potentially addictive personality. Luckily, and probably because of my parents' problems, I *was* aware of it. I quickly tired of the fast lane, and while in my life I would make other mistakes, I sidestepped the big one: substance abuse.

I have an idea that may help if you have any concerns

at all about your partying—whether you are young or old, but especially if you are young.

It's hard to know just how much you are drinking when you are in the party crowd. You wake up the next day with a hangover or maybe even a complete lack of memories of the night before. But can you honestly say how much you drank? One night I found out, almost by accident. I was having drinks, and after the first one, I stuck the little "drink pick" in my back pocket. Then someone bought the whole crowd double drinks. I thought, *Well, I'll save those, too.* As the night went on, I continued to stow away those picks reflexively.

The next morning I groaned, got out of bed, and grabbed my jeans from the floor. The back pocket was stuffed with those plastic picks—*stuffed*!

I saw the fine line I walked, and while I never have been a complete teetotaler, I have remained aware and careful about what I drink. Being the child of a legendary drinker adds an extra layer of complexity to the alcohol question.

One night when I was in Nashville staying with my dad, a woman in a bar asked me if I wanted a drink, and I declined. She asked again.

"Oh come on, have a drink."

Once again, I said, "No thanks."

And again, she pressed the issue.

I finally explained that I was staying out at Dad's and didn't think I should show up with liquor on my breath. The woman looked at me as if she thought I was a nut.

"George Jones? George Jones! You're George Jones's kid and you don't want him to smell alcohol on you? He certainly shouldn't have anything to say about *that*!"

I stood there for a minute and then excused myself.

"I think I'll wait for you in the car," I said to a songwriter friend. "When you're done talking, we'll go."

I was too young, inexperienced, and nonconfrontational to know what else to say. But while I sat in the car waiting, I felt like kicking myself for not cussing her out. I felt like I should have said, "First of all, I'm the only one who can talk about my dad. And second, how the hell do you know anything about him? Except some oldies you've heard? And last, he is my daddy! You may not respect your own daddy, but I respect mine, and I'm not gonna show up at his house smelling like booze."

And it got me thinking about what it must be like to be Daddy. Everyone expects him to pass around the bottle. Everyone wants to buy him a drink. When he doesn't have a drink, it becomes a big issue. No wonder he'd rather be home watching football on television.

COMING OF AGE means many things for many people. For me, it meant finding the gumption to finish my senior and junior years of high school in one year, to recognize my inclination for substance abuse, and to begin to understand both parents, for better and worse. Most important, it meant beginning to see myself as a separate entity from either one.

PART FOUR

Losing My Mother

Nineteen

IN THE PROCESS OF FINDING myself, I briefly lost my mom. When I dropped the divorce bomb in the late fall of 1990, the news blindsided Mom. She had no idea that my marriage was falling apart, and I didn't really try to explain what had happened, the patterns that had led to talk of divorce. A lot of our problems had been the partying, and I was a participant in much of it. Moreover, while he had cheated on me, I had paid him back by cheating. It would take me some years to learn that one betrayal does not justify another.

I had learned a lot, though, and made changes. But what could I have told Mom? It took time for me to sort out the lessons. In hindsight, I could have explained that both of us were partying too much and that I was concerned about my own tendency to drink. I could have told her how hurt I was to learn of his infidelity and that I was ashamed of my own.

I didn't say any of that. No real explanation. I couldn't have articulated it at the time, even if I'd wanted to do so. Not unless I wanted to bring up my own failings. Communication skills were not among the areas of my newfound personal growth. I didn't insist that we sit down and talk it out or try to explain. Instead, I dug in my heels and decided that if Mom turned her back on me, then I would do the same. I just kept my head down, so it appeared to Mom that I hadn't given my marriage a chance, and that I hadn't worked at it. When she accused me of making a rash decision, I talked back to her. It was the first time I had ever done so.

Mom sometimes flipped back and forth between being very lenient to almost excessively firm. She hated being the disciplinarian, never wanted to be the parent that had to come down hard on her children. But when she *was* strict, she could be as hard as MeeMaw had been with her. What transpired was almost a replay of what had once happened to Mom. At first, MeeMaw had been against her marriage to Euple Byrd, but when Mom decided to leave him, MeeMaw was infuriated and turned on her. And so it was with Mom and me. We didn't speak for months. Hardheadedness on Mom's part and on mine caused the divorce and its aftermath to be a terrible time for both of us.

But in a strange way, that falling-out paved the way for a better, more complete relationship, one that continued until the time Mom died. Though we never spoke of it, the two of us were determined never to become estranged again.

FINDING ANOTHER HUSBAND had been the last thing on my mind. But when I thought my first husband was being unfaithful, I turned to a coworker at the hospital where I was employed part-time while attending nursing school. Joel Smith was everything that my first husband was not. Whereas Billy was a big kid out to have fun, Joel was mature, responsible, and serious-minded: husband material. Joel was in the Army National Guard, a medic just deploying for the Gulf War. He knew what he wanted to do in life and was willing to work hard to see it happen. It was a good match. Both of us saw ourselves as working in the medical field, having a family, and maybe even having that white picket fence that my mom and I both coveted.

Money was a problem for me when I divorced Billy. Mom had been helping me with nursing school. But at that point, she didn't offer financial assistance and I didn't ask for it. I stayed at Joel's apartment, where his rent was paid up, until he returned home from the Gulf. I used his car, and with the rent paid, I just had to make enough money working in the emergency room to pay for utilities, gasoline, and food. I ate a *lot* of ramen noodles. Joel was back in the States six months later.

I didn't go home for Thanksgiving or Christmas in 1990. I didn't call Mom, and she didn't call me. I had never missed one of those celebrations before. Yet even the missed holidays didn't cause us to mend the relationship.

The situation changed the following year when MeeMaw's health, already very bad, took another downturn, and she came to stay with Mom in Nashville. Bottom line: if I wanted to visit MeeMaw, I had to make up with Mom. When I finally bit the bullet and phoned her, I could hear the relief in her voice, and I'm sure she could hear it in mine, as well. All it took was me coming home once for us to put it all behind. We didn't talk about it. We just moved on.

I've thought hard about what had happened between Mom and me. I loved her so much, and her refusal to stand with me during a hard time did hurt. But you can choose to deal with things by dwelling on how they might have been, or you can face them as they are.

I remember a conversation that Mom once had with PeePaw. This anecdote doesn't have anything to do with mending relationships, but it's an interesting way of looking at things.

PeePaw had arthritis in his hands, and one of them especially caused him pain from time to time. Years earlier, he'd broken that hand and never seen a doctor. It healed wrong, and over the years caused the hand to curl up just a bit. It also contributed to his arthritis pain. Mom worried about this and often talked about it to me and to others in the family. Then one day she finally sat him down and had a talk with him.

"I want to take you to my doctor and get you on some pain medicine," she said. "You don't have to hurt like this."

PeePaw politely turned down that offer, possibly because he saw what doctors passing out pain medicine had done to Mom. But Mom wasn't finished. She thought that if he wouldn't take pain medication, he should see a doctor for a permanent solution.

"Well, I think, then, that you should let me have your

hand fixed," Mom went on. "They can rebreak that bone, and when it properly heals, you'll feel a lot better. And I think that you'll have the full use of that hand again, too. It won't be crippled up anymore."

PeePaw gave that some thought.

He was old, and the idea of going through a surgery on the chance that he could have nimble fingers wasn't one he relished. He finally got a little twinkle in his eye and said, "Aw, honey, my hand just now fits the steering wheel."

I think that sometimes that's how you have to look at the world. Once in a while, you simply have to be glad your hand finally fits the steering wheel and get on down the road.

My way of "getting down the road" involved finishing my nursing degree. I had started my classwork at Auburn in September of 1990. But in January of 1991, I enrolled at Southern Union, which is a community college in Opelika, Alabama. Always in a hurry, and now short of funds, I liked the idea of a sooner-rather-than-later graduation date. Auburn was a four-year program offering a bachelor of science in nursing (BSN), while Southern Union offered the shorter associate degree in nursing (ADN). Both degrees qualify the individual as a registered nurse. I had been working in hospitals ever since I started my training, and most of the nurses I knew said there was little or no difference in the pay scale that they could see. The BSN was preferable if you wanted to go into research, administration, or become a physician's assistant. I had no desire to be in research. I wanted a hands-on nursing job. And I knew that if my goals changed, I could always go back to college and finish a four-year program.

There was another element in my decision. I'd noticed some elitism at Auburn. A few of the instructors spoke in derogatory terms when they talked about nurses with associate degrees, saying that they were not "quite" as qualified. I'd worked with nurses of both kinds and disagreed with that assessment. I started checking out the differences and realized that the only class I couldn't get at Southern Union was in statistics. And more important, Southern Union had an even better rate of nursing graduates passing the state boards. Once I changed schools, I was doubly happy with my choice. The classes were smaller and the faculty was more approachable. I graduated in December of 1992 with my ADN. Mom came to my graduation, so proud, she was just glowing.

IN SOME WAYS, a separation with Mom had begun around the time I decided to finish high school early. That's when Mom and Richey discovered they were in financial trouble over bad investments and chose to move. Not moving with them was my first real declaration of independence, a distancing. Beyond that, I think for Mom and Richey, moving to Nashville had been more about leaving Florida than getting back to Tennessee.

If Mom and Richey had hoped moving back to Nashville would distance them from the Florida mess, they could not have been more wrong. Not only did the problem follow them to Tennessee, the bad publicity probably intensified because they were in Music City. Mom hated to let anyone—even her children—know about her finances. So when her money woes were plastered all over the Nashville papers, it was almost unbearable.

In September of 1988, federal marshals came to Mom and Richey's home with a court order to take possession of the house and its contents. This was the original Franklin Road house, called First Lady Acres, the house she'd got when she divorced Dad.

It all had to do with two loans totaling $750,000 from a savings and loan, which was by then out of business. The money had been used to invest in two shopping centers that had also gone down the drain. Some of the S&L's officers had been indicted for fraud. The only thing that saved Mom from losing everything was bankruptcy, with the downside that all her business was put right out there for the world to read. One of the most embarrassing things that came to light was a $50,000 loan Mom had taken from Burt Reynolds. That just killed her—having people know that she'd had to take money from him.

I don't know if the shopping center investment was part of the shady dealings Mom was worried about when she dragged my sisters into the infamous briefcase affair, when Mom thought Richey was keeping business secrets from her. Jackie posed that question in *Tammy Wynette,* the book she wrote in 2000. It was clear that business decisions were being made behind Mom's back and that she was unhappy about them. It's a question that will never be answered, though. Mom's wall of secrecy over most money matters was in place until the day she died.

The crazy thing is, even when Mom and Richey started scaling down their lifestyle, things didn't change on a public level. For example, Mom thought they should sell the big house on Franklin Road, but when they did, Richey decided to buy yet another big home on the same street—

this one with an even more prestigious address than First Lady Acres. It had once belonged to Hank Williams, a fact that Richey often shared when talking of the move. Mom wasn't even that pleased with the house, saying she no longer had reason to own a big place, given that her children were all grown.

But down the road they went to Hank's house—Mom's final move.

Mom and Richey got a good deal on the Williams house, which had been bought and sold several times and was in foreclosure. And whether or not the purchase made financial sense, Richey found the money to not only buy the house, but to start remodeling. Of course, as long as Mom stayed the workhorse in the family, they could always find ready cash.

Mom was intrigued with the history of this house. Hank was one of her heroes, and the fact that he'd lived there meant a lot to her. Furthermore, she loved Franklin Road. It was close to Music Row, where she did business, but isolated enough for privacy.

Once again, she jumped right in the middle of decorating mania. The house needed a lot of updating, so she was back to meeting with interior designers and making trips to furniture stores. I think her top mission was to create the perfect home for the Christmas season. She wanted all the holiday bells and whistles, the heavily decorated trees, garlands, and sparkling lights. She wanted everything decorated the day after Thanksgiving. So while some people were running around shopping on that big Friday after Thanksgiving, Mom was knee deep in ornament boxes. And of course, all the sparkle served as the backdrop for

Mom's Christmas dinners—which were what she *really* loved putting together.

Mom's health was in flux throughout the late '80s and early '90s. When she tried to kick reliance on pain medication at the Betty Ford clinic in 1986, she suffered a severe bowel obstruction, had to have surgery, and ultimately ended up at the Mayo Clinic. It was a rough time for Mom's pride because she tried to avoid admitting to weaknesses, and she hated being the subject of Music Row gossip. To check into Betty Ford was to admit to a problem and to demand that industry tongues start wagging.

What a tumultuous time for someone who guarded her privacy as much as Mom did—bankruptcy, federal marshals, Betty Ford. The Mayo Clinic stay revived her, though, and she came back to Nashville ready to record and to tour. It was a good thing she wanted to hit the road, because Richey constantly pushed her out there. It was the only way to straighten out their finances.

In 1989, Mom hit the road with Randy Travis and the Judds, sponsored by GMC Trucks. Mom couldn't have been happier because she loved Randy Travis—absolutely adored him. It was more than his voice, too, although she thought he was one of the finest male vocalists she'd ever heard. What Mom appreciated about Randy was his old-fashioned—almost courtly—ways. He was almost a throwback, treating women like grand ladies. She also came to see Wynonna Judd as a daughter figure. Times when Wynonna and her own mother, Naomi, were at war, Wy hid out on Mom's bus. Mom became her sounding board, friend, and surrogate mother.

Mom was a great fan of the Judds, and especially of

Wynonna's voice. She loved that big Southern gospel element that Wynonna has and appreciated her passion. Another younger singer she always loved as both a person and an artist was Tanya Tucker. The first time Mom ever heard Tanya, when she was thirteen and working in the studio with Billy Sherrill, she said she was overwhelmed by the raw talent and maturity Tanya displayed.

The tour with Randy Travis was a great success, serving to bolster Mom's self-confidence as she was moving into "that certain age" when female stars are not always considered bankable. Given the severity of her health problems just a couple of years earlier, it's amazing that she could still wow audiences. But she did.

In 1991, Mom made a career move that shocked country music. It started when she received an invitation to sing with a British pop-rock duo called the KLF. Mom had never heard of them, but their proposal interested her. She told Jackie she did it "for fun."

The duo came to Nashville and recorded a song called "Justified and Ancient," and then took everyone back to London to make a video. And what a video it was! The duo (Bill Drummond and Jimi Cauty) dressed up in robes and rhino masks, while Mom was outfitted in a crown and a mermaid dress. They added Zulu dancers and turned the whole thing into a strange, mystical spectacle. If not for the end result, people might have questioned Mom's sanity, and some probably did anyway. But her instinct was to go along with the project and have a good time, even though she remained clueless about the point of it all.

"Justified and Ancient" was a hit in eighteen countries, expanding Mom's worldwide icon status to a generation and audience that had never heard of "Stand by Your Man." So while it may have seemed like she was indulging herself on a whim, the KLF project was a savvy move.

THAT SAME YEAR tragedy struck the family when Aunt Carolyn's youngest child died. Kriston Jetton was just a few weeks younger than I, born in 1970. Mom thought of Kris as one of her own children and his death devastated her.

Kris was born deformed: his intestines were on the outside of his body, he had no fingers or toes and only a hint of a nose. Kris had more than a hundred operations as a child in attempts to build fingers or toes, and to fix his misshapen face. He was a tough little guy. Doctors said he would never be able to walk without leg braces, but by the time he was seven he proved them wrong. Kris was one of the biggest gifts our family ever had.

I was close to him as a child. As an adult, I still admire him more than nearly anyone I have ever met. He was very smart and interested in everything. He was funny—enjoyed jokes and having a good time. And he loved going to school even though he was often teased and bullied because of his physical appearance. Despite the taunts, Kris could always find something to smile about. He participated in Boy Scouts and other extracurricular activities. No amount of finger pointing or snickering could keep him from getting involved or making the most of every opportunity.

I've thought about that quality of his so many times through the years, because I didn't have it. I didn't stand up so well in the face of bullying or teasing. Someone could pull down my spirits in a heartbeat. If Kris's spirit took a beating, you never saw it.

Kris could do something else that I found difficult. He had an innate ability to know what to say when someone was hurting. I can still picture him at Carolyn's funeral. The two of us were only eight years old. He was so young to have just lost his mother. People were trying to hold it together for the sake of Kris, as well as Carolyn's other two children, but Mom could barely control her emotions. Kris had been watching her sitting there, shaking, with her eyes straight ahead, trying not to cry. Just before the service started, Kris walked over to Mom and put his arm around her.

"Don't worry. Mommy's better now. She's an angel."

It truly was an amazing moment. Through all his own sadness, Kris had reached out to someone in need of help.

Kris and Mom had a running joke about noses. As I mentioned earlier, Mom hated the fact that she had "the Russell nose," which had a bump. Kris, of course, had almost *no* nose.

"I wish I had the Russell nose," he'd say to Mom.

"I wish you had *my* Russell nose!" Mom would say with a laugh.

But over the years, Kris continued to talk about his lack of a nose, and Mom realized that beneath the gag was a burning desire to have something done about his facial features. One day she sat him down and they had a long talk about it. If he still felt that way when he turned eighteen, Mom said she would pay whatever it took to get him the nose he wanted.

"I just want to make sure you've stopped growing, so the surgery can be done safely," she said.

The day Kris turned eighteen, he called Mom and said he was ready. This was right in the middle of Mom and Richey's financial trouble, but she didn't care. And while Richey often tried to control every cent she spent, I think he knew better than to cross her on this expenditure. Off they went to find the best plastic surgeon they could. That doctor performed a miracle on Kris. A plate was implanted in his head, giving his face shape where little had existed. Then the doctor built a nose and cheekbones. He looked almost like any other eighteen-year-old walking down the street. Not quite, but close enough for Kris! He was thrilled.

Kris told Mom that he'd never felt such self-confidence, that people no longer cringed when they saw him or looked at him with pity. He also told her how much she had meant to him all through his childhood. He never once felt she saw him as different from anyone else; she wasn't pitying and never once drew back from him as so many did. But of course, that was Mom. She truly didn't see him as a damaged person. She saw the beautiful spirit he had, and she loved him for it.

A year or so later, Kris had some seizures. The doctors worried that they had been caused by that plate in his head, and so they removed it. It didn't destroy the new face he'd received completely, though, and the seizures stopped. We thought taking out the plate had taken care of everything, and that there was no concern about Kris's life being in any danger. But it was.

He was a twenty-one-year-old college student when he died. One morning a friend noticed that Kris hadn't been to his classes. Oversleeping and missing class was not something he did. If anyone appreciated the opportunity to attend college, that person was Kriston Jetton. The friend knocked on his door. No answer. When he finally went inside, Kris was on the floor beside his bed. The coroner determined that he must have had a seizure in the night and fallen to the floor. By the time he was found the next morning, he'd been dead for hours.

Mom paid for his funeral and made sure it was a wonderful tribute to him. A lot of people came that we'd never met, people Kris's courage and heart had touched at one time or another. I had so many thoughts about him that day, his determination, his outlook. I know if he had lived, that he would have made a difference in the world—his spirit would have inspired everyone he met. It was a wonderful day of remembrance, but also a day of great loss.

And as it had been with Carolyn's service, Kris's funeral was one Mom almost couldn't face. She had convinced herself that the surgery had killed him. All she could think about was that the plate in his head had brought on that first seizure. I tried to tell her that no matter what caused the seizures, Kris had wanted that surgery and believed it had changed his life. He loved having his new face. But for the rest of her life, Mom blamed herself for Kris's death.

TWENTY

WHEN JOEL SMITH RETURNED FROM the Gulf in 1991, we started planning a wedding. We decided to try to pay for as much as possible ourselves. I was well aware of the financial problems Mom and Richey faced through the failure of those shopping mall investments and the resulting bankruptcy. Plus, after the falling-out I'd had with Mom, I felt more comfortable standing on my own feet. We decided to hold the wedding in Tuskegee, Alabama, where Joel's family lived.

I borrowed a wedding gown and some bridesmaid dresses from a friend. Our friend Guy was sweet enough to offer to buy flowers for the church and decorations for the reception. Guy ended up making the food for the reception, too. I had been determined not to ask Mom for anything, but she insisted on paying for the preacher. The only money Joel and I ended up paying was his tuxedo rental and $500 for wedding photos.

I asked Mom to give me away. After she met Joel and saw the same steady character traits in him as I'd seen, she was fully supportive of our plans. I didn't trust asking Dad again, because I figured he would turn me down. I sent him an invitation to the wedding, but he didn't come.

I hadn't been sure how Mom would take the invitation, since walking someone down the aisle was considered a male thing to do. But she was thrilled and looking forward to it. That made it doubly hard for her when she became seriously ill and was taken to the hospital the day before she was to leave for Tuskegee. She called in tears from the hospital, feeling like she'd let me down. I tried my best to assure her that it was fine and that all we wanted was for her to get well. Gwen stepped in and walked me down the aisle on June 13, 1992, at a rural Baptist church in Tuskegee, Alabama.

We decided not to have a honeymoon, but to start saving for a quick trip to Six Flags in Atlanta, only two hours away. As far as I could see, this was a good way to start married life: sane, sober, and responsible. Our first order of business was to start a family. Both Joel and I wanted babies—as soon as possible. My body, however, didn't cooperate.

My first pregnancy was ectopic (tubal). Then I went through six months of taking increasing doses of fertility drugs, until Joel and I moved to Birmingham, Alabama, for new jobs. There, I began going to the Kirklin Clinic at the University of Alabama at Birmingham (UAB). The doctor at Kirklin was concerned that my Clomid dosage to induce ovulation was too strong, and reduced it from 150 mg to 50 mg. I was also taking injections of hormones because I'd had an ongoing problem with irregular menstrual periods. The doctor told me to go home and wait a month. At that point, I'd be put on a new medication.

I went home discouraged, worried that I would never be able to have a baby. I waited the full month and returned, even though the hormones should have made me start my period. The doctor looked over my chart and suggested we give it a few more days before we tried another injection. Nothing happened, and I wondered if I'd ever have the regular periods I'd no doubt need to conceive. I was so upset and moody! Then my breasts started feeling sore.

Hmm, I thought. *Well, a pregnancy test can't hurt.*

Of course, it *could* hurt—and *had* hurt many times over the past year or so when I'd hoped to get a positive but didn't. I seemed to become more depressed with each negative result.

Sure enough, the test showed negative. But this time there was also part of a positive sign, just a light shade that represented about half of a positive. Joel called the doctor as soon as he got home from work, and he instructed us to come in for a blood test. We did, and then got a message to come back for a *second* test. I was getting so confused and nervous. They were looking for the levels of HCG—cells that nourish fertilized eggs—that would tell them if I might have had a miscarriage.

Unbelievable! The levels were right. I was pregnant!

"We've got to go right back for an ultrasound," I told Joel.

"What? Already?"

"Yes. If this is another ectopic pregnancy, I don't think I can stand it. I want to know right now if it's going to break our hearts again."

Joel was with me when I got the ultrasound, and the two of us looked at each other with fear when the technician started mumbling, seemingly confused. "Well, a baby, uh, well . . ."

The unspoken question between Joel and me was, Is our baby all right?

Finally, the young woman doing the test spoke a coherent sentence. "You're having twins."

Sure enough, there on the screen were two dots, what looked like two little eyes staring back at us. We ran straight back to the apartment to call Mom. These wouldn't be the first "twosome" in the family. Jackie had given birth to fraternal twin girls in February of 1988. After a lot of shrieking and laughing, she said she could not believe that Jackie and I had both given her two babies at a time to spoil! I thought about calling my dad but decided it could wait. We hadn't talked lately.

My ob-gyn explained that twins would mean a different process than a single-birth pregnancy. I would need more ultrasounds and other tests, especially as we got to the third trimester. He said that early birth was common for twins, and so we needed to be very careful to try and prevent that for as long as possible. The twins were due in December 1993. When I started spotting early on, the doctor told me I had to get some bedrest. Since the hospital took a hard line on missed days because of pregnancy complications, this put my job at UAB at risk. I quit the job at UAB and went to work at Brookwood Medical Center in Birmingham.

I had two baby showers. One was organized by my friends in Alabama, the other in Nashville by Mom. We held them early in the pregnancy, since no one knew if I'd be able to go full term. Mom's guest list was typical. She invited the people she was close to on a day-to-day basis—no stars, just the people she worked with and whom I'd known when I was on the road with her: stylists, hairdressers, band members' wives. And of course, there were my sisters, cousins, and Richey's family. As it turned out, having the shower early was a smart move.

I was in my sixth month when I started feeling a tremendous amount of pressure in my abdomen. When I went in to check it out, the doctor said I was 90 percent effaced and fingertip dilated. By the time they gave me a shot to stop early labor I was having contractions every two minutes. I was sent home with instructions for complete bedrest. The only time my feet were supposed to hit the floor was when I took a shower or went to the bathroom. With Joel having to be gone every day, I was worried and scared. But a few days after I'd let my family know what was going on, there was a knock at the door, and there stood Mom.

I was unprepared for Mom's decision to come to Alabama. She had been touring heavily and had finished work on a new album with Dolly and Loretta: *Honky Tonk Angels*. Mom had laughed that Dolly pushed them into it by saying she was determined that the three of them recorded together before one of them died!

That October, when I was having problems with the pregnancy, not only did Mom come to Alabama to see about me, she came to work. She cleaned and cooked and babied me. She told me stories about when my sisters and I were born, when Jackie's twins had been born, and any other baby stories she happened to think of. I'm surprised I didn't pop considering how much I ate. Mom cooked country-fried steak, gravy, biscuits, potatoes, fried okra, corn bread, banana pudding. She made meals for us to freeze and eat later. Mom stayed three days before she had to leave and get back on tour. But she told me that she had insisted on taking the entire month of December off to help me when they were born.

Having her there was like wrapping myself in a warm blanket. I felt safe, convinced that everything was going to be fine. Mom had that effect on me. As long as she was there, I felt nothing could hurt me, nothing could really go wrong. And having her there without Richey was especially good. It was just the two of us.

But not long after she went back to Nashville, the pressure started again. The doctor told me to take one dose of my medicine and come to the hospital if I had any more than six contractions in an hour. I took the medicine and waited. The contractions continued. Surely, this couldn't be happening. I was still six weeks away from full term. It was in the early hours of the morning, and when I heard a bang on my door, I realized that my neighbor was delivering newspapers. I made it to the door and gasped, "I'm in labor. I've got to get to the hospital."

She and her husband rushed me in and called Joel. I told them to tell him to stay at work, though, because at that point I believed the doctors would be able to stop labor with more medication. They were not. Even the IV drip didn't stop those contractions.

"You better call your husband," the doctor advised. "Those twins are coming."

I called Joel, then my mom, who freaked. She had an interview scheduled that hour, and then was supposed to leave the very next day for a month's tour in England.

"Don't worry," she said. "I'm coming right after the interview. I'll have to leave for England tomorrow, but I'll be with you today!"

The timing wasn't perfect. Kyle Everett Smith was born on October 26, 1993, at 1:50 p.m. (weighing 4 pounds and 13 ounces), and Joel Ryan Smith was born at 1:54 p.m. (5 pounds and 3 ounces). Mom got to the hospital about an hour later. She spent a few minutes with me and then ran down the hall to see her new grandsons. The next morning she was off to Europe—with grandbaby photos.

Mom had called Dad and Nancy before she left Nashville, and they sent a huge bouquet of flowers to me in the hospital. Along with the arrangement came a note congratulating Joel and me and welcoming Kyle and Ryan to the family. They had twin cribs delivered for the boys.

It made me think of the first time Nancy came to Mom's house a few years earlier, dropping off presents for Jackie's twins. Mom was so nervous about Nancy's visit. She made sure everything was spotless, that she looked good. Later she confessed that she'd spent a lot of time feeling jealous of Dad's new wife. But as they were around each other, both developed a liking for the other, and respect as well.

Nancy encouraging Dad to visit Mom in Baptist Hospital earlier that year had solidified the friendship. It was important to Mom that I understand and allow Nancy into my heart as well.

"She's really very nice, Georgette. Nancy and I have become friends. I like her a lot." Then she thought about it and added, "I believe she is perfect for your dad. He's lucky to have found her."

Mom really led the way for me to change the way I treated Nancy. I had resented her, there's no getting around that. I tried to call them from time to time after they were first married. But I rarely got through, and that made it easy for my bitterness to grow.

I made the mistake of listening to tale-carrying people who tried to place the blame for me not seeing Dad on my stepmother. Some told me things that Nancy had supposedly said, including that she was behind Dad's not attending my first wedding. I also heard that when Dad had given me a car for my sixteenth birthday, Nancy didn't think I acted appreciative enough. I later figured out that many things attributed to Nancy were never said. Other comments were taken out of context or simply misunderstood. For one thing, I *knew* the truth about Dad refusing to walk me down the aisle at my first wedding: he hadn't attended that wedding because he was mad about me not listening to him.

Still, I knew that Dad wasn't going to hop on a plane to come see his newborn grandsons. He first met the twins when they were nine months old. Joel and I heard that Dad was playing a show in Montgomery, Alabama, and we decided to go. We spent time on the bus both before and after, and Dad was genuinely moved by meeting Kyle and Ryan. But although we all pledged that we'd stay in contact and visit often, we still spent little time together over the next several years.

The twins were about a year old when Nancy phoned me at work with the news that Dad had to have heart surgery. I think the fact that he and I hadn't been in good contact during the past few years made me all the more determined to be with him. Joel and I made arrangements at work and left immediately with the boys for Nashville. We stayed several days, until we knew Dad was out of the woods.

When Dad started feeling better he told me that Waylon Jennings had explained what all to expect after the operation. Waylon told Dad to be ready to feel a little scared when he first came out from under the anesthetic.

"But, Hoss, you won't believe how good you're gonna feel in just a few days."

Dad said Waylon had been right, that he was starting to feel like a new man. He also told me that Waylon said the worst part of the whole experience was the chest tubes.

"When that little nurse started pulling the first tube outta me, I thought she was never gonna finish!" Waylon said. "I told her that it seemed like she was pulling the crank on a lawn mower. That first one took so long that I told her the second one belonged to me, and she might just as well leave it."

I also talked to my aunt Helen, the sister that used to try and protect Dad and his mother from George Washington Jones's drinking bouts. She told me more about Dad's childhood, and I tried to understand more about why he so often held back affection from me. With Dad, it all goes back to trust.

THE YEAR THE twins were born happened to be the year Joel and I were scheduled to have Thanksgiving with his parents. I thought I'd die without Mom's food, and so did Joel. By that time he, too, was addicted to her home cooking. One day just before the holiday, a package came with the entire meal packed in dry ice.

Mom had included turkey and her famous dressing, the one that she supplied for holiday meals even when we went to other people's homes over the years. The dressing wasn't the only thing she was known for. We always looked forward to having her homemade biscuits during our visits, so she made a big batch, then froze them; all we had to do was pop them in the oven. Tina and I always loved Mom's cheese potatoes, so she included those, as well as green beans and homemade strawberry jam. The whole meal was topped off with two of my favorite pies, pumpkin and sweet potato. We left a lot of the food frozen, and Joel and I dined on it for months.

Between new babies and Mom's home cooking, my life seemed great. At the same time, Mom seemed to be reinventing herself at every turn. She played Carnegie Hall in New York in April of 1994, sharing the stage with such diverse artists as James Taylor, Elton John, Aaron Neville, and Luciano Pavarotti. That same year she recorded *Without Walls*, a duet album with a lineup that included, among others, Elton John, Wynonna, Smokey Robinson, and Cliff Richard. Elton John, especially, loved Mom. He autographed a photo of himself for her with this inscription: "To the Queen of Country Music. From the Queen of Pop."

Mom framed it and displayed it proudly on a wall.

Then, in 1995, Norro Wilson and Tony Brown produced one last duet album with Mom and Dad, titled *One*. Both had been through health setbacks in the past few years, but they sang beautifully. And by this time, the two of them were good friends.

TWENTY-ONE

ONCE WE HAD THE TWINS in 1993, Joel and I decided to save some money by moving to Tuskegee and living in a trailer on his parents' property. All we had to do was take care of the mowing and the goats! We desperately needed to keep expenses down, because Joel had gone back to school. He was already a licensed practical nurse, but we both believed he'd be better off to finish a nursing program to become an RN, a registered nurse.

We planned our schedules so that one of us could be with the boys while the other worked. The only time we needed a babysitter was on the one weekend a month that Joel had army drill and I was at the hospital. By 1995, when the boys were eighteen months old, we enrolled them in day care two days a week so we could expand our work hours.

I think that our working so much and trying to divide time taking care of the boys caused us to begin to grow apart. We didn't see each other as much as we probably should have to keep building a marriage. I would be coming home just in time for Joel to walk out the door. Even when we had time off, we were usually going in opposite directions. Joel began to want to stay at home almost anytime he wasn't working.

The problem became more complicated when Joel no longer wanted to make the drive to visit Mom in Nashville. Because I refused to lose touch with Mom, the boys and I started making the drive alone. Mom and I used to laugh at how I could turn into some sort of Super Stretch person groping around on the floor of the backseat for a dropped pacifier, while keeping eyes on the road. It took me six hours to make what was normally a five-hour drive.

One of those trips proved to me that Mom was the one who could turn "super" when taking care of babies and toddlers. At one point in 1994, Mom thought it would be fun for me to go to lunch with my sisters while I was in Nashville, and she volunteered to keep our children. It was an astonishing offer when you consider that I had the twins, Jackie had four youngsters, and Tina had her son. That meant seven small children, including two sets of twins. At first, we turned down the offer.

"What are you girls talking about?" Mom said. "I raised four babies! Take your time and have fun. Have lunch. Go shopping. Just have some sister time."

We were nervous about it but decided to take her at her

word. If Mom said she could do something, we had to believe that she could. When we returned several hours later, Mom had my boys and Tina's son down for naps. Jackie's two older girls were watching television, and the younger two were coloring. And Mom had dinner on the stove!

Those were the times that I told myself that rumors of her continually taking too much pain medicine must be wildly exaggerated. Obviously, we wouldn't have left those children with her if she'd been even slightly incapacitated. She had been fine for the whole visit.

One thing became more obvious with each visit—Mom had to account for every cent she spent. When it came to money, she felt that she had to answer to Richey. Never mind that she was earning the money, he was in charge of finances. During those trips to Nashville with the boys, I had often found myself smiling to myself when Mom said, "Let me give you some cash." She'd start digging in her purse, and come up with some odd amount of money. Thirty-two dollars. Sixty-eight. Twenty-seven. It was never an even number.

"I'm fine, Mom. I don't need it," I'd say. (All of us girls knew that if we really needed help, we could go to her.)

"No, no," she'd say. "I want to give you something. Maybe this will help with gas."

When she was determined to buy us something, she tried to hide the purchases. If we went to a shopping mall, and she insisted on buying me some clothes, we never took the packages out of her car. They stayed in her trunk until she could slip them into my car unnoticed. If she'd used credit cards, she'd try to make sure she was around when the bills came. That included her own clothing bills unless

Richey had been along and in control of what she purchased. "Control" is the operative word here. I remember one time in '95 when he put her on an allowance.

"You can't be serious!" I said, when she told me.

"Well, you know," she said with a shrug.

It wasn't always possible to do, but I tried to stay away from conversations like that. I never wanted to get tangled up in one of those Mom-and-Richey messes. But there was one very troubling episode when I did speak up, and it bothers me to this day. I came home to find her sitting on the couch in the kitchen, crying.

"What in the world is the matter?" I asked.

She shook her head. "Oh—Richey and I argue so much. And this time—" She stopped. I could tell that she didn't really want to get into this conversation. Mom and Richey had a lot of problems, and she'd wanted to leave him several times over the years. But I hadn't seen her quite so low before. "What happened? What did he say that's upset you like this?"

She stared down at the Kleenex she clutched in her hand. Finally, she said, "He told me that all these years we've been married have just been a waste of his time."

I knew that he talked like that to her, and that her self-esteem was getting worse almost on a daily basis. A waste of his time! That really angered me, but I knew better than to act like I was mad. I sat down beside her on the couch.

"Mom, you don't have to live like this. You don't have to be so unhappy. You can leave him."

She shook her head. "No, I don't have anyplace to go."

"That's just silly! This is *your* house. *You* paid for it. But aside from that, you could come live with one of us girls. You have so many friends! You could stay with any of them until you decide what to do. We can leave right now."

"No. I can't leave him. He's already told me what he'd do if I left."

I certainly don't know what having your blood boil really feels like, but right then I think I came pretty close. "And just what is he going to do if you leave?"

Mom hated cussing. She didn't care if anybody else cussed, but she'd been raised to never swear or use inappropriate language under any circumstance. So when she finally spoke, I nearly fell off the couch. She looked stricken even as she opened her mouth. I knew the words pained her terribly.

"He says he'll write a book and tell the world I'm a 'fucking druggie and a whore.' He says he can destroy my life and my career. And it *would* destroy me. People all over town would be laughing at me."

"I don't believe that," I said. "People would know he was just trash-talking. People love you too much to take him seriously."

She shook her head. "They love what they think I am. Georgette, I've had a lot of men in my life. I've been married five times, and every one of those marriages was a failure. People believe I finally found love. I just can't stand the thought of being humiliated like that."

I knew she'd been taking too many medications and that she was no doubt addicted to them. Maybe he could accuse her of that, although he was the one who administered the meds. But if he had her convinced that having five marriages made her a whore, I knew he could convince her of anything. I stayed with her until I heard Richey drive up. There was no talking her into leaving or even confronting him on those threats. She wouldn't, and she wouldn't allow me to do it.

MOM CALLED US all into the living room during the Thanksgiving holidays of 1996, saying that she had something important to discuss. All four of us girls were there, as well as Richey's kids, Deirdre and Kelly.

Mom appeared so serious that she nearly frightened me.

"I want you all to know about my will," she began. "I don't want another Conway Twitty kind of fiasco happening when I'm gone. I don't want you kids or Richey wondering what it is that I want."

Conway's children and third wife, Dee, had been involved in a very public dispute over his estate, and Mom had been horrified by the public nature of it all.

Several of us protested, telling her she didn't need to justify or explain anything she had decided.

"No, I want to say this," she insisted. "I want everyone concerned to know what I've done so there won't be any misunderstandings. I want to go over everything."

Mom said that we first needed to know that she had taken out two life insurance policies, each for $1 million. On her death, one would go to Richey and the other to the kids. She said that Richey, as her husband, would get the house and business, until his own death, at which time everything would come to us. She reminded us that she had all the lists of specific gifts that would come to each of us, things we'd agreed upon over the years. Her yellow legal pad had become legendary in our family. Every so often, she'd sit us down and go over them, the lists of treasures from her house and life. Everything from her crystal collections and Oriental carpets, to the china sets, jewelry, career memorabilia, and furniture was included on those lists. They seemed endless. She changed them from time to time, if someone decided they'd rather have a different framed award or a necklace they'd not mentioned before.

At times, Mom almost seemed frantic that everything was written down, that every item anyone desired was accounted for. It was very important to her that the grandchildren also be included in her lists, even the ones too small to have any specific requests. She wanted things to be equal, so that no one felt they'd been slighted. Those considerations were very important to her, that each of us feel we'd been treated fairly.

None of the decisions had much to do with what each item was worth. Mom's tastes were all over the place, and so were ours. Her crystal figurines ranged from very expensive pieces she bought when she was on tour in Europe to something she saw at a five-and-dime for a few dollars. If it caught her eye, she displayed it right beside museum-worthy items. Of course we all wanted to have our own baby books, and we'd go through boxes looking at family photos to find specific ones we might want or need to have reproduced.

Each time Mom went through one of her list episodes, she seemed to feel relieved. I know that having everything in order was important to her. Her yellow legal pad was always around, always close at hand.

"I'm watching out for this list," she'd explain.

• • •

MY MARRIAGE WAS rapidly disintegrating through 1996. Joel and I had been concerned that our work schedules were distancing us, but our problems ran much deeper. Something drastic had changed after the twins were born. Joel was thrilled with the boys, loved them as much as any father ever loved his children. But I guess he started seeing me as the twins' mother, not as a wife. It took a while for me to realize what was going on. Childbirth, followed by the around-the-clock work of having two babies, kept me overwhelmed for months. By the time I started feeling like myself again, Joel was no longer interested. A distance between us began to grow, and it was physical in addition to emotional.

He also had experienced some problems adjusting after coming back from the Gulf War, and although post-traumatic stress disorder was not talked about much then, I believe he suffered from it. He had started drinking more than he should and was getting moody. This was another case of two people not communicating at the very time when conversations are crucial.

But the lion's share of the problem existed between Joel and me, and was about our lack of intimacy. Joel didn't even kiss me, except for an occasional peck on the cheek. He simply was not interested. At one point, we went ten months without having sex. I started feeling more unattractive and inadequate by the day.

I became one of those women who have a marriage in name only, who do nothing but work, take care of the kids, and fall into bed exhausted every night. Over time, my one relief was making that drive to Nashville where I could spend time with Mom and my sisters. I said nothing about my marital problems when I was in Nashville. The last time I'd covered up marriage problems, it was because my first husband and I were both acting like immature party animals. This time I was silent to protect my husband. Mom sometimes turned into a mother lion when it came to her cubs, and in case we worked things out, I didn't want her to hate Joel.

I was ripe for making a mistake. Finally, I was so starved for someone to tell me that I was attractive, to show some interest in me, that I began seeing another man. I'm not justifying, just explaining. And like so many country songs, my life was about slipping around, lying, and covering up—cheating on my husband.

I'm not proud of it.

It didn't take long before Joel suspected that I was seeing someone and hired a private investigator to follow me around. I should have known that something was going on. Joel started encouraging me to go out with my girlfriends, gave me money to do so even when we were short on cash. Yet I was oblivious to the fact that I was being investigated.

My own guilt in the divorce takes nothing away from Joel's problems. Even his mother knew he was going through rough times that involved far more than my actions. Down the road, she helped him financially as leverage to get him to stop drinking and start going to church. And her strategy worked as near as I could tell. I think she helped pull him out of that dark place he'd been.

It didn't have any effect on how he saw me—any physical feelings he'd had toward me were long gone. That didn't mean that our divorce was easy, or that he just shrugged and walked away. He was mad about me running around and planned on making me pay for it.

We ended up in a custody fight that presented a new set of worries. My boyfriend was an African American, and we were in the Deep South. I knew that while the South wasn't as discriminatory as in years past, everything might depend on one man—a judge—and his personal attitudes. The man I was seeing isn't the type to want publicity or have his name brought up in any public airing of my infidelity, so I will just call him "David."

The thought of me being painted as a bad mother killed me. I was a very good mother, just a bad wife. I started getting paranoid and began to wonder if Joel had just wanted me to have his children, then get out of the picture. Dragging out my tale of woe wasn't going to do me any good, either. I doubted that a court cared *why* I started cheating on my husband.

The only person I could turn to was Mom. I hadn't talked to her about my troubles. So once again, I knew that I would be springing something new on her—something that might cause her to turn away from me. But this time the stakes were much higher, so I was willing to beg if necessary.

I phoned Mom and told the whole story, start to finish. I came clean about my affair and told her I was worried that we might have a racist judge. I explained about the private investigator. And I asked her to help me get an attorney. It was a lot for Mom to take in all at once. But she certainly never made me beg. She got right in the middle of it.

"Don't worry, Georgette," Mom reassured me. "I'm not going to let you lose those boys."

I've heard speculation that Mom was upset that my boyfriend was a black man. I'd like to make it clear that she was not. She did worry that David and I would face discrimination. The 1950s South that Mom grew up in was very different from the 1990s. But in spite of a few sly glances, the only race problem David and I faced happened later that year, when we were in the North.

Once Mom heard my story, she went into full mother lion mode. She had her Nashville attorney find me a good lawyer in Tuskegee, and then she had Richey bring her to Alabama for court, just in case I needed a character witness. Gwen came as well. Every one of them came—including George Richey—ready to talk about me having been a good mother and explain that I was the primary caregiver for the twins.

In the end, no one had to testify. The morning we were scheduled to be in court, the lawyers worked out a joint custody agreement. I would keep the boys for seven days, and then Joel would have them for seven days. Every other year we would swap holidays. There was no child support as such, but each of us paid for one of the twins' school expenses. Then, all doctor fees and other expenditures were split down the middle.

The resolution happened so fast that I never did have the opportunity to introduce Mom to David. No problem,

I thought. I'll bring him to Nashville soon, and they can spend some time together.

It didn't take long for everything to begin to unravel.

Joel remarried not long after our divorce was final in 1997, and his wife seemed to want to take my place in the boys' lives. They had a house with a yard for the boys, whereas I lived in an apartment. Moreover, I was seeing the same man I'd had the affair with, but we had no plans to marry.

I was scared to death and had no money for another lawyer. I thought about going to Mom, but she had already stepped in to help, and I doubted Richey would allow it again. I was afraid that if I became a "problem child" that Richey could easily convince her to steer clear of me. That I could not face.

So I tried as best I could to present the picture of "the good mother." I rented a more expensive place, a real house instead of just an apartment. I tried to dress better—tried to look like a typical middle-class mom. I used makeup more than I usually did, going for that soccer-mom image.

All it did was make me more insecure and depressed.

I started feeling like I was a complete loser, as a woman, a mother, a human being. Then this depression of mine started spiraling down to even greater depths. I hadn't been able to connect with my dad for months, and I started thinking that somehow my lack of worth was to blame for that as well. I wasn't any good as a mother or a daughter.

Depression is a dangerous thing. You can convince yourself of almost anything. I started thinking that my sons might be better off without me in their lives. What if Joel's wife was right? What if I was a negative to my own children? The only answer for me, then, would be to kill myself.

I even had the means to do it. When Joel and I got married, I had purchased a LadySmith 9mm for my personal protection, a lightweight Smith & Wesson pistol. One of my classes in college, an ROTC course, had provided excellent training with that gun. I knew how to shoot. I'd been a nurse far too long to ever try to kill myself with pills. Too many times those suicide attempts go bad—and the person is left alive but unable to care for herself. I certainly didn't want *that* to happen. If I decided to kill myself, I didn't want to be left with a messed-up brain.

One day I stood in my bedroom and looked at my gun. For the first time I understood that I had been negotiating with myself, trying to excuse suicide by justifying the use of a gun instead of some other method.

Dear Lord! I thought. *I am about an inch away from killing myself!*

That's when the enormity of it all really hit me in the face. If I committed suicide, my children would have the action hanging over them for their entire lives! I knew that I could neither do that to the boys, nor could I completely trust myself not to stay depressed. And so I carefully took the gun, put it in my purse, drove to a pawnbroker, and sold it. I threw away the pawn ticket and never seriously looked back—not even when suicide seemed like it might become a viable option, as it soon did.

Twenty-Two

IN MARCH OF 1998, MOM'S hairdresser called to tell me that Mom had been admitted to a hospital in Pittsburgh. Although I later learned that Mom thought my sisters and I had been told, Richey kept the news from us. He said it was because he didn't want any press coming around bothering her. I had some days off work right then, and because the twins were with their dad, I decided to surprise her with a visit.

"Please don't say a word about me coming," I said. "Don't tell Mom and don't tell Richey."

I knew that if I even hinted that I was coming, Richey would tell me that Mom was probably going to be discharged before I could even get there. That was what he usually said. I wasn't sure how long it would take, either, because Pennsylvania is a long way from South Alabama!

David said that he felt like he ought to drive up with me. "We can take turns driving so you can get some sleep." He was right. It would have been a long, long drive to make alone. And it seemed like a good idea for another reason. Mom hadn't met David, although she knew I'd been seeing him. She wanted to meet him for a couple of reasons. First, she just wanted to know the man I was seeing. Second, she wanted him to know firsthand that she had no problems with our relationship.

She couldn't stand bigotry or stereotyping people. Minorities who were discriminated against were not merely an oppressed segment of the population to her. Other races, the gay community—those were people she counted among her friends.

So it was not because of race that David decided he should stay in the waiting room while I first visited with Mom. It was because I had not seen her in some time, and we weren't sure just how sick she was. Also, David worried that Mom would hate to meet someone for the first time while in a hospital bed and probably without her makeup and her hair fixed—looking very un-starlike. Moreover, neither David nor I looked all that great after the long drive, and he wasn't excited about meeting Mom looking like he needed a shower and a shave.

I finally decided to play it by ear. Given the time it took to drive, I wasn't sure just how long I'd have with her. I didn't know how she'd be feeling. So we determined that David would wait downstairs for the time being.

Richey was surprised when I walked in the room, surprised and obviously irritated. Mom was happy that I'd come. After we'd hugged and talked a little bit, Richey got up and said in something of a sullen tone, "Well, I'll get out of here and let you two talk."

We had a wonderful visit. I put lotion on her feet and filled her in about the twins, my job—and more about my boyfriend, David. I did let her know that he'd come with me, because she was worried about me driving such a long distance. When she asked why he hadn't come up, I told her that he had come to see some friends in Pittsburgh and was picking me up. I could tell she was getting tired, so I told her I needed to get back and wait for him to pick me up.

On my way out, I ran into one of the doctors who'd been treating her. It was a great relief when he told me that, in his opinion, there was nothing to worry about: "She's in good shape, her tests are coming back fine." Then I returned to the waiting room. David sat in the same place I'd left him, but he looked nearly sick.

"Before anything else happens, Georgette, I want you to ask this couple what just went on," David said.

The couple who sat just behind him looked upset. "Ma'am, this is all very strange. Some cop just came over here and told your friend he was going to have to leave. All he'd been doing was watching a basketball game on television!"

"What?" It made no sense to me, and I said so.

"I'm worried," David said. "I didn't think I should leave, because you wouldn't know where I was. I told the policewoman that I'd been waiting on someone."

"What did she say when you told her that?" I asked.

"Get out. She just said *get out*."

I looked around, and suddenly it hit me. He was the only African American in the entire waiting room. He *did* look like he needed a shave and a shower. But of course, there were several white people who looked like they'd been through long drives or waiting periods, too.

"I'm a little worried about leaving, Georgette. I'm thinking that if she sees me with a white girl, this is going to get ugly. She may try to say I'm some kind of druggie or something. I think we should call the room and have your stepfather come down here while we go back to the car."

"No, no," I said. "That's not going to be a problem. Mom and Richey have a good relationship with these doctors and nurses. I'll just call security and let them know we're here seeing Mom and are leaving."

That's how naïve I was about how race can change things. This was 1998. I thought the bad old days were over. We'd just come from Alabama, where we'd never had a serious problem. We'd had people stare and even make comments. But there had been no incidents. Plus, we were in Pittsburgh. This was the North, for Pete's sake! So I went looking for a security guard. I spotted an office just around the corner from the main waiting area. They let me use the phone, and I called Mom's room. Richey was back, and he answered.

"Look, Richey, I think you may need to come down here to the waiting room. Some police officer has tried to kick David out, and we're nervous about going back to the car. Maybe you should talk to someone."

"Oh, okay." Richey didn't seem to think it was going to be any big deal.

I hung up the phone and turned to see a policewoman

and a male security guard standing there listening to my conversation. I don't know why, but I didn't snap to the fact that this must be the policewoman in question. I guess I was just too exhausted to think straight.

The policewoman looked me up and down. "Do you have some kind of a problem?"

"Yes. A friend of mine needs help in the lobby."

"Your friend is causing problems and needs to leave," she said.

Oh, no, I thought.

"Are you visiting someone in the hospital?" she asked.

"Yes, I was visiting my mother."

"Are you planning on visiting her again?" The woman looked at me as if I were some kind of scum, and it was only then that I knew exactly who she was. She was the problem. I thought I'd better start back toward the room and meet Richey.

"Yes, I think visiting my mother again is a very good idea," I said, and started to walk around her. She stood there, blocking me.

"Well, I can't leave with you standing there in the doorway," I said. I know that I should have been more careful in my tone of voice, but I'd never been treated that way before. I was in that hospital visiting my own mother!

The woman stepped back just a little, but as I started to go around her, she shoved me—actually pushed my shoulder into the doorjamb. I remember thinking, *This isn't happening! This kind of thing happens on TV!* Once again, I reacted before thinking it through.

"Don't touch me! You have no right to touch me!" I said in a loud voice.

"You get out of this hospital right now," she hissed. "Get out before I arrest you."

That really got my back up.

"I'm not doing anything until my stepfather gets here and we resolve this," I snapped. "I haven't done anything wrong!"

"I am a City of Pittsburgh police officer," she said. "If I tell you that you have to leave, then you have to leave."

By this time, I was afraid to leave for the car. When I didn't move, the woman shoved me again. We went out into the hall, while she pushed and shoved, then slammed me against the wall and snapped on the handcuffs. When we started out the waiting room door, David jumped up. I frowned and shook my head. That's *all* I needed, David to step into the middle of the mess. He stood there staring at me. I just hoped he knew that Richey was on his way down.

It was very cold, thirty or forty degrees.

"Call the wagon," the officer said to the security guard. "This one's going to jail."

Then she slammed me onto the pavement, face-first.

"Why are you arresting me?" I cried out.

"Trespassing," she said.

"Trespassing! How can I be trespassing at a public hospital?" I was still being stupid. I thought I had the right to ask questions.

"Assault."

"I didn't assault you! I didn't even touch you! You pushed me!"

She knelt down until her mouth was about an inch away from my face. "Shut up. If you'd touched me, I'd have broke your fucking neck. I'd have bashed your skull in."

I decided she was right. I better shut up.

Meanwhile, Richey came into the waiting room, and David recognized him. He told him as much of the story as he knew, and that I'd been taken out in handcuffs. Richey ran out to the parking lot.

"Back up!" she ordered.

Richey stopped walking. "Where are you taking her?" he called.

The woman started laughing. And she never said one word to Richey. Just hauled me into the police wagon and slammed the door. I tried to think the incident through while I was sitting there in handcuffs, traveling through the streets of Pittsburgh. I believed—and still believe—that what prompted the entire episode was the fact that David was a young black male who looked somewhat disheveled from a long and tiring drive. When I interjected myself into the situation, it was perceived as questioning her authority. Richey showing up in the parking lot just made her madder. I think by then she was determined to ride this out as long as possible, and the best way to do that was to take me in and book me.

I later learned that when Richey got back up to Mom's room, she phoned her doctor, who gave them the number of a high-powered local attorney. Then Richey took David with him out to Mom's tour bus sitting in the parking lot. The two of them waited for a message from the attorney, while Richey fielded phone calls from Mom. David said that every time she called the bus, he could hear her frustration level rising.

"Have you heard anything?"

"Has that lawyer called?"

"Can't you do something?"

"Richey, what is happening to my baby? Call and find out what is going on, *now*! This is ridiculous! *I want to know where she is!*"

I was in jail. I was taken to a precinct station house, where I got a mug shot, got fingerprinted, and was placed in a holding cell. For the first time in my life, I had some understanding of what it felt like to be powerless. I'd never even thought about it before. It occurred to me that David had been right when he said he feared walking out to the parking lot after having words with an officer. It could turn very ugly, very fast. There were a lot of things rolling around in my mind right then—thoughts about race and the justice system—but the biggest thing of all was a very personal fear.

The cell smelled terrible. Feces had been smeared on parts of the wall and on the side of the toilet, which sat right out in the open where anyone—other inmates, guards, and visitors—could see. By that time, I really needed to pee, but I held it. Aside from the filth, too many people were walking around outside the cell. A male inmate came by and handed me a paper bag containing a bologna sandwich, some lemon cookies, and an orange drink. My stomach hurt, and I couldn't even think of eating or drinking. Plus I still needed to pee.

A policeman walked down the hall, and I frantically waved to him.

"I want to make my phone call."

"What phone call?" The policeman seemed amused.

"Don't I get a phone call?"

"You've been watching too much television!" The officer laughed out loud. "You'll get a phone call when you need a phone call."

"I *do* need a phone call! I've got to call my ex and tell him to pick up the kids from school—"

But the guy had walked on down the hall. I really did need to call my ex. It was getting late. He would take the kids to school the next morning, thinking I would be back to pick them up. I started feeling desperate, thinking of them standing there waiting on me, on their dad, on *someone*! I wondered what Mom and Richey were able to get done about me, about what they'd even been able to find out. And I worried about Mom having to deal with this while she was in the hospital. I kept thinking it would have been better if David and I had just tried to sneak out of the waiting room and get to the car, if I hadn't tried to talk to *anybody*.

The next time anyone stopped by my cell it was to bring me a roommate, one who seemed to know her way around. That guard wasn't interested in my phone call or child care issues, either. The clock kept on ticking. Nine-thirty p.m. and nobody came.

"You better hope we get out of this holding cell before midnight," my new roommate said. "It's Friday, and the judges won't hear any cases between Friday midnight and Monday morning. If that happens, we'll be strip-searched and taken to general population."

Just when I thought it couldn't get any worse!

This young woman didn't seem much like a criminal, either, so I asked her that age-old jail question: *What are you in for?* She explained that she had borrowed a friend's car to take her little boy somewhere. She'd been pulled over by a police officer who knew her *and* her ex, who was a police officer. She said that they refused to call and check out that she had permission to drive someone else's car. They'd said that until they got it sorted out, the car would be considered stolen. She was a nurse, an LPN.

"Anytime some of my ex's friends see me driving, I get pulled over," she said, seemingly resigned to the fact. According to her, the ex-husband had been abusive, but she finally gave up calling the police when she was hurt, because all they did was go outside and talk to him. Then he'd come back angrier than he'd been in the first place.

I kept thinking, *This isn't real.* I am in jail, hearing more about the police than I wanted to know and starting to question everything I ever believed. What happened to *the police are your friends*? I really wanted to get back to South Alabama.

It took six hours for the attorney to get me released.

The first thing I did was to call my ex-husband and make sure he picked up the boys the next day. I didn't tell him that I'd been in jail. I was afraid that unless I explained the whole thing in person, he would have a fit and file new charges against me. I just told him that I needed to stay longer because of Mom's situation. I hated lying about it but was just too freaked to think of anything else. Then I called Mom at the hospital, where she was waiting for news. It was late, so I decided David and I better get on the road.

We couldn't get back to Alabama fast enough.

Only when I learned that the story of me getting arrested was going to be in the tabloids did I decide to confess to my ex-husband. By the time I finally talked to Joel Smith, I knew that the tabloid was portraying me as some kind of drug-crazed lunatic. I knew that my dad would see the tabloid, and I would be an embarrassment to him—but the idea of losing my boys overshadowed all else.

Joel was hesitant in his response. It sounded like such a crazy story, something so nutty that there had to be more to it. But in the end, he said he didn't believe that I'd attack a police officer, that I had been on any drugs—*or* that I was crazy.

"Let's let this sort itself out," he said, finally.

I was so relieved that I nearly fainted.

Mom and I spoke on the phone a few times in the next few weeks. She was concerned that I was doing okay emotionally after the arrest, and I was concerned that I'd embarrassed her. My mug shot had been in the *Star,* making it look and sound like I was demented. And the police officer had filed suit against me personally on the assault charge, saying I had attacked her and caused permanent bodily harm. That just stunned me. I was the one who had been shoved against the wall. That officer outweighed me by a hundred pounds! I couldn't have done her any bodily harm if I'd tried!

I knew that I needed to get my stress levels down before my court date, so I started taking inventory about all I could and *could not* make happen. Mom was a big help with that endeavor. For one thing, she knew that I wanted to get rid of my GMC truck payment, so she got Richey's brother Carl to trade it in at a car auction for a Geo Prizm. That was typical Mom, very practical, knowing that getting the payment down by a couple of hundred a month would make all the difference.

I saw her one more time, when the boys and I came to Nashville right after she returned from Pennsylvania. Her health appeared to be okay, so I thought that the doctors had been right. She was going to be just fine. But in retrospect, she seemed to know something was different when we said our good-byes. She was always sad before she said good-bye to any of us, but this time she held me a long time, crying. I tried to reassure her, saying that I'd be back soon. She still clung to me, and then stepped back with an incredibly sad look on her face.

When I got home from Nashville, I had a call from my attorney in Pittsburgh. He told me that my day in court over the Pennsylvania arrest was shaping up to be a big win. I decided to wait and tell Mom about it the next time I drove down.

TWENTY-THREE

MAYBE IT'S WHAT A HOME invasion feels like. You hear something outside that gets your attention but doesn't really scare you. Then suddenly someone kicks in your door and the nightmare starts. It was almost 10:30 p.m. on the night of April 6, 1998. I was working the second shift at Russell Medical Center in Alexander City, Alabama. Second floor, medical-surgical wing. Thirty minutes more and my shift would be over. I heard a noise and realized someone had walked into room 281, where I was hooking up a patient's IV.

"Do you need any help?" the charge nurse asked, reaching out as if to take the IV tube from my hand. Another nurse who had followed her in the room turned off the television.

What in the world are they doing? I wondered.

"No, I don't need any help." I was probably a little short, because I can almost hook up an IV blindfolded. Plus, you don't just walk in and take over someone's job. I finished taping up the IV. They kept standing there, looking uncomfortable.

"Can you come out in the hall with me for a minute?" the charge nurse finally asked. "I'll check back on your patient."

I followed her out of the room, confused. The pitying yet urgent look on her face suddenly frightened me.

"Georgette, you need to go home. Right now."

Oh God! "My kids! Has something happened—"

"No," she said quickly. "Your kids are fine. But you need to call your mom's house."

"What's happened? Is Mom all right? My sisters?"

"You just need to call." She kept right on walking, and I could see that she did not want to be having this conversation with me.

I took her arm, insisting that she turn and face me again. "Look, I need to know—"

She sighed and looked like she was ready to cry. Then she said that one of our colleagues had just phoned the nurse's station. "Jenny heard that your mom died today and called to find out if you were all right. She thought you'd probably already left for Nashville."

That had to be wrong. I started to contradict her, in complete denial. "No—"

"I am so sorry. But it's on the television. They said Tammy Wynette is dead. It evidently happened earlier today."

On the television? Earlier in the day? It made no sense. Someone would have called me if Mom died many hours ago. Everyone knew where I worked. If I hadn't answered when they called my house, they'd have tried me at work. It had to be some terrible mistake. Maybe something happened and my stepfather had to call an ambulance. Maybe one of the neighbors saw the flashing lights and called the local news without knowing what had happened.

I called Mom's number. George Richey's sister-in-law, Sylvia, answered the telephone. I was nearly frantic to talk to someone.

"Sylvia, what is going on? Someone just told me that Mom passed away!"

"Yes, honey, she did." And then silence. Nothing. I waited for some kind of explanation, some information. But there was just silence.

"Are my sisters there?" I asked. "Is Tina or Jackie or Gwen there?"

"Do you want to talk to one of them?"

"Yes!" I sure wanted to talk to *somebody.*

"The only one I can find is Tina," Sylvia said.

"Fine! Of course I'll talk to Tina!" I answered.

I thought I'd made it clear that I didn't *care* who I talked to.

About the only thing Tina knew was that our mother had been dead for hours. She didn't know what had happened. When I asked why no one had let me know, Tina said she thought our sister Gwen had called. I nodded numbly. Maybe there was a message on my home phone.

"I'll start for Nashville now, Tina," I said, and hung up.

I went to my supervisor to say I was leaving, and honestly, that's what I thought I did. In fact, according to the records, I didn't actually check out. I just left. The administration knew what was going on, but still, you'd think *I would have realized* what I was doing.

The person I did call was my ex-husband. I explained to Joel what had happened and asked him to talk to the boys the next morning. Joel and I agreed that awakening them for bad news would be more stressful than anything else. Joel said he would let them know later. This was hurting him, too. Whatever our problems may have been, Joel cared about my mom. Then I phoned David.

I recall looking down at my charts before I left, thinking that I was leaving a mess for the next shift. That was so unlike me. I always tried to have everything in order. Nevertheless, I just grabbed my purse and ran to the parking lot and the green Geo Prizm. David was at the house when I arrived, and by the time I threw a few things in a bag, it was nearly 11:00.

"I don't want you making that drive alone," he said. "I'll take you down to Nashville. I don't want to get involved in all this, but I *will* drive you."

Even with David doing the driving, I'd never felt so alone on that road to Tennessee.

I tried to think back to the last time I'd talked to Mom's doctor. "She's in good shape, her tests are coming back fine." That's what he'd told me. I knew people perceived her as a tragically ill woman. Pain from many surgeries had aged her a lot over the last several years. But while she had health issues, she wasn't terminal. I still worried about the medication she took, but her doctor had said she was under the care of a top pain management facility. She'd been recently checked. Her blood work was good. *Better than she'd been in years.*

All I could think about during the drive was that I'd let Mom down. For years, I had tried to do the right thing, failing at times, succeeding more often than not. But a month before that night, I'd wound up splashed all over the tabloids in stories that made me sound crazy. I'd gone to jail and been fingerprinted, had my mug shot published in newspapers throughout the country.

Mom stood by me through it all, a tower of strength at a time when I was further down than I'd ever been. I had no idea what my father thought about the tabloid stories. I hadn't talked to him in over a year and believed that whatever relationship we'd once had was gone forever. So I wrote him off.

My trial was coming up in just a few months, and I knew Mom worried about it. I had been thinking of making a trip to Nashville so she could see firsthand that I was doing okay. Why had I put it off? *Why* hadn't I called her the previous week, just to let her know that I was okay? My attorney had convinced me that I'd be acquitted. Surprising information had surfaced, damning evidence against the officer who'd filed the charges. I should have let Mom know about the new development. Did she die worried that I would be convicted of assaulting a police officer—that I might do prison time?

I wanted to explain that my life hadn't turned into a train wreck. It had seemed like it might at first. I lost my job with the Home Health Care Services. They couldn't have someone with outstanding assault charges caring for homebound patients. But I had found a nursing job at Russell Medical Center. Mom knew I'd found another job, but she didn't know how much I loved the hospital and the people I worked with.

After fearing that I might lose custody of my boys after the arrest, my ex-husband and I had finally come to a workable agreement about joint custody. By working the 3:00 to 11:00 shift, I could collect extra pay, which meant I could just cover my bills each month without running to Mom for help. I worked seven days on, and seven days off, so I could be home with the boys.

Standing on my own two feet was important to me. I was Mom's frugal daughter, saving my allowance, paying attention to the jobs I did around the house to earn the money, even negotiating for a raise when I felt I deserved one. I'm not saying I enjoyed the childhood chores, but I did take the duties seriously. And I always wanted to make my mother proud of me.

Yet there it had been just months earlier—my police mug shot in the *Star*. And as David drove me down Interstate 65 on the night my mother died, those tabloid headlines stretched out in front of me as sure as the highway. As numb as I felt, my mind raced, jumbled with scattered thoughts about Mom. It didn't seem like she had left the world. Certainly not my world. Not yet, anyway. I could feel her arm around my shoulder, hear her voice when we got on the big carnival rides: *Don't be scared, Georgette!*

But when I turned on the car radio, I was reminded that today's horror was all too real. The country station was playing Tammy Wynette songs to mourn the passing of a star. I finally had to turn it off. Somewhere along the road, we decided to check into a motel when we got to Nashville. It would be nearly 3:00 a.m. when we got there. Surely, everyone at the house would be asleep. For a little longer, in my mind, Mom would still be there.

The house on Franklin Road *was* Mom. The two things you first noticed when entering the front hall were the chandeliers and Oriental carpet, her two greatest household extravagances. My sisters and I used to kid her about how much she loved her chandeliers, how she loved having them all turned on, glittering like Christmas throughout the year. She'd found them all over the world, just as she did her carpets.

As I had predicted, it was after 3:00 a.m. when I saw the lights of Nashville in the distance, twelve hours since I'd started a seemingly uneventful shift at the hospital. David pulled off the interstate in Brentwood and checked us into a motel. Even though I spent most of the night staring at the walls, I have no memory of the room. It might have been fine, or it might have been a dump. It didn't matter, because everything was just a blur. I finally slept some between 5:00 and 6:00, then took a shower and got dressed to go to Mom's house.

The drive was already filled with cars when I arrived at Mom's at 7:00 a.m. I parked at the back of the line, wanting to both run inside and to run away. It took five or ten minutes of sitting there alone to get my nerve up. I went inside, and it looked the way it always did—the Oriental carpets, the chandeliers, the cases filled with crystal figurines, gold records on the wall. And there were the melon drapes she'd picked out against her decorator's advice. As I looked around, I saw so many reflections of my mother's life. But she was missing.

Some of Mom's friends were there, and my stepfather's relatives. My stepfather, George Richey, sat crying, seemingly inconsolable. I tried to get more information about the actual cause of Mom's death, but no one seemed to know much. The Davidson County Medical Examiner hadn't even been called. Richey had flown Mom's doctor in from Pittsburgh, and he'd pronounced her dead. They also told me that Mom had been lying dead on the couch for hours before anyone noticed she was not breathing. Then she lay there hours longer before the funeral home finally took her body away at 1:00 a.m. My sisters were upset that when they arrived the night before, people were going in and out of the kitchen, getting coffee, making sandwiches. And all the time Mom's body was lying cold on the couch. When they could take it no more, they shooed everyone out and shut the door to give her some respect.

I couldn't believe that they had to *insist* that people treat Mom's body with respect!

I stood looking at the couch where Mom died and listening to Richey's sobbing. I remembered one day just a year or so earlier when I stopped by the house and found Mom crying.

It all came flooding back—that time when Mom told me that Richey had threatened to tell people she was a drugged-out whore. I started to fill with anger all over again.

I stood looking at the couch where we'd had that conversation, knowing that it was where Mom had drawn her last breath. But I also knew that I couldn't start getting mad all over again about something that had happened in the past, because the *right now* was almost more than I could deal with.

It finally dawned on me that I'd brought nothing to wear to a funeral. So I asked around and found someone who had a dress I could borrow. I wore the same size shoe as Mom, so I thought I'd go look and see what I could find. I thought I should let Richey know that I was going up to her closet, even though he still seemed so upset and was almost incapable of carrying on a conversation. The change was immediate and shocking.

"Be sure you bring them back, Georgette," he said in a crisp, businesslike tone. "I'll need absolutely everything in this house appraised."

Once I'd had that conversation with Richey, I wasn't sure quite what to do. I started feeling incredibly lonely, almost frightened, despite the fact that my sisters were there, that Mom's friends kept asking if I was all right. I felt like I was a visitor and that the woman who'd died in that house was being separated from me, taken away all over again.

I went out into the big hall and stood in the corner. I kept seeing Mom in my mind, doing cartwheels and backbends to entertain my sisters and me at First Lady Acres. Mom—laughing and making us laugh. She was such a funny woman, and I suddenly felt incredibly sad that so few people knew that side of her.

More people had started arriving. I didn't really want to talk to anyone or try to be sociable. I stopped paying attention to what was going on in the front entry and stood there staring down at Mom's Oriental carpet. I remembered how proud Mom was that she'd been able to buy fine things for herself, that she'd earned her own way in the world.

All of a sudden, I heard the door open and close, and there was an immediate change in the air, electricity. I glanced over my shoulder and there stood George and Nancy Jones. You'd have thought the Pope had walked in. People gushed over him while he stood there looking like a deer caught in the headlights. I refused to look directly at him, sure that it hadn't been his idea to show up. Dad hated anything to do with deaths and funerals, and I thought he just came because Nancy believed he was obligated to do so.

Nancy took charge of the crowd around him and soon dispatched everyone. Then she walked over to me and took my arm.

"You go talk to your father, Georgette," she said firmly.

I shook my head and started to turn away. I was too on edge to face one more emotional conflict. "I jus—I just don't think I can, Nancy," I stammered.

She didn't let go of my arm. "Don't turn away from your daddy. Don't you know that he's worried about you? That he's hurting, too? You are the reason he's here!"

I turned toward him, and the look of pain on his face was startling. I went toward him, not sure what to do or say. He met me halfway across the room and put his arms around me.

"I'm so sorry, honey," he said, his voice breaking. "I love you so much."

I'd never needed to hear my father say *I love you* as badly as I did just then. For the first time since I'd heard that my mother was dead, I started to cry.

And as I stood there in my daddy's arms, crying for my mom, somehow I felt a healing begin.

PART FIVE

Finding My Father

TWENTY-FOUR

BY THE TIME MOM DIED, I had just about written Dad off for good. I saw him now and then, but it never seemed quite like what I believed a father-daughter relationship should be. Just about the time I'd start thinking we were close, he'd drop out of sight, once again convincing me that he just flat out did *not* care about me.

Truthfully, I don't think I'd have my dad in my life today if he hadn't made the first move right after Mom died. And even when he did, we had to start with baby steps. I kept thinking that too much time had gone by for us to be father and daughter. I remained fearful and suspicious, just waiting for the inevitable letdown. Finally, I asked myself, "What if I'm standing at his funeral one day wondering why I hadn't kept trying?"

What kept me going was Dad—he hadn't given up. He hadn't quit. He was willing to come to the house of bereavement and try to help me when I needed it most.

I didn't know just how badly I would need him that week Mom died. Almost from the moment I'd walked into the house on Franklin Road, I had felt like an interloper at my own mother's death. George Richey's treatment of me, my sisters, and the memory of our mother was abominable.

First was Richey's attitude about me borrowing a pair of Mom's shoes. Had I heard that right? Had my stepfather actually demanded that I account for the shoes I'd had to borrow for the funeral? Had he actually said that he needed an accounting of everything? This was the man who had been sitting in the hall for an entire day howling with pain over his wife's death? And now he's trying to figure out what a used pair of shoes is worth?

Then there was how he treated various people. For example, when my father entered the house, Richey put on a show for all to see.

"Oh, Lord, help us! Lord, how we are gonna miss our Tammy!"

But as soon as everyone had witnessed him going on and on to George Jones, Richey was back in the office going over funeral and visitation plans in businesslike tones. I noticed that his most professional conversations were about the public memorial, the one he knew was being covered by television cameras.

When it came to the *details* of death—the ones that didn't involve television ratings—Richey just wasn't up to the task. That's when George Jones had to step in. It's hard to know whether Richey just didn't want to deal with something as mundane as picking out a casket or whether he had taken so many drugs that he was physically unable to do it. He certainly seemed drugged up. I guess Dad and Nancy realized that we would have no help from Richey. That is when they stepped up to the plate, offering to go with us to the mortuary when we chose a casket. They stayed with us through the entire process, never trying to influence us, but they were there for any advice we needed.

We did talk about the fact that Mom had an aversion to being buried underground. She did not want it to happen. Dad stood by us when we suggested that Mom be buried *above*ground at Woodlawn Cemetery, on Thompson Lane in Nashville, where she was to be interred.

Only family and very close friends were supposed to be coming to the visitation the night before the funeral. So I was surprised to hear Richey talking to first one and then another celebrity on the telephone, inviting them to come by and pay their respects to Mom. I worried about it, about how she would look to the public, so my sisters and I, along with Richey's daughter Deirdre, decided we would dress her. At least we would be able to get her ready for the viewing. I hoped we were up to the task.

Mom's appearance would have horrified her. Let's face it: Mom was a vain woman. She always wanted to look nice, and the aging she'd done over the past few years had upset her terribly. Yet there she was—her face so swollen that her lip had cracked open. I guess I had always seen people either at the funeral—when they had been worked on for hours—or just recently passed at a hospital or nursing home. But I had never seen someone who had been left to swell until her face was cracking open and it couldn't be fixed.

Yes, Mom had lain there on that couch so long after death that the swelling was distorted, almost impossible to conceal. I had been a nurse since 1992, yet nothing could prepare me for seeing Mom look this way. I hated the fact that other people would be seeing her looking so awful.

When I first saw Mom, she was "dressed" in a clear plastic jumpsuit sort of thing, covered by a sheet. That's how I will forever remember Mom—in that plastic jumpsuit and with a cracked face. I was nearly sick at the thought of anyone else seeing her that way.

What made it doubly tragic for me was the finality of it. I hadn't been there when the body was removed, so seeing her just prior to the official viewing meant I finally had to face reality. Mom was dead. Not just dead, but horribly and disfiguringly dead.

We dressed her, although I don't know where we found the strength. We somehow made it through the visitation, and it was on to the first of two funerals on April 9. The smaller, private funeral came first, held that morning at Judson Baptist Church. That so-called family service was when I first started to believe that Richey was specifically distancing himself from my sisters and me. We—the immediate family—were to wait in a small sanctuary until the church was filled with relatives and friends. But Richey wasn't around. He walked in before the service started and, thankfully, remained fairly quiet. I did see Dad and Nancy in the crowd, and we nodded. Somehow seeing them there gave me comfort. But when the service was over, we were swept back to the house to prepare to go to the "main event"—the public memorial at the Ryman.

For anyone who ever asked me what being the child of a celebrity was about, let me say that Mom's public funeral combined what constitutes the lowest and highest points. First, there is no doubt that it warmed my heart to see the people who came from all over the world to pay tribute to Mom. Those fans truly loved her, and that meant a lot to me and to my sisters. But the flip side was hearing Richey on the telephone, bragging about the event being as big as Princess Diana's death. The difference between him on those phone calls and him when he sobbed to the stars in attendance or for cameras was obscene.

I hadn't had a chance to talk to Dad before the smaller funeral. If I had, I would have asked him to sit with David and me at the Ryman service. David had agreed to come with me, even though he felt very uncomfortable in the middle of what seemed almost like a circus atmosphere. To hear Richey tell it, everything was about the "show" and the "ratings"—none of it had much to do with Mom.

Driving through the crowds had a big effect on me. As I watched people crying or waving to those of us in the funeral procession, I was impressed at how much respect they all showed, how much love they seemed to have for Mom. I was still a little too numb to feel much, but the warmth those people displayed was almost like an arm around my shoulder.

Dad and Nancy also came to the Ryman service, sitting in the audience with everyone else. Once again, as soon as I saw him there, I felt I could make it through the rest of the day. I remember thinking that it must be the first time I had ever sat out in those audience seats. I'd always been backstage with Mom. Just as the fans had given me strength, words from Randy Travis and Dolly Parton were bittersweet.

The words that jarred me, causing my ears to feel hot and (I'm sure) turn pink—came from the preacher. He got up and said, "Tammy has left the building."

I hated that. It made Mom's death seem like some show business cliché. Then what was already bad turned worse. With the help of his son and Lorrie Morgan, Richey got up to speak. He rambled, cried, and practically needed to be carried off on a stretcher. What he did in public was far different from how I'd heard him in the home office, speculating about funeral ratings and how Tammy would stack up against Princess Di. Here is exactly how I felt: it was as if his fake pitifulness was mocking me—making a mockery of the pain that I and my sisters felt. I felt nauseated by him.

Finally, I leaned over and whispered to Jackie: "If he doesn't sit down in a couple of minutes, I am going to walk up there and snatch him down myself."

Of course I didn't do anything of the kind. It was already a big enough spectacle.

I was relieved when it was all over. I spoke briefly to Dad and Nancy, who let me know that they were there whenever I needed them, and then I stood in almost a trance while people stopped by and talked about Mom. These were people I should have known, but many I didn't.

David Keith talked with me that day and told me how much he loved Mom. I'd seen him among the people milling around after the service, and he looked familiar. But I drew a blank that day. It was only later, when I watched a video of the service, where people were identified by the television commentators, that I understood who he was. Luckily, I ran into him several years back and was able to tell him how much I appreciated his coming to pay his respects to Mom. I told him that he was one of her favorite actors and that she had loved him in *An Officer and a Gentleman.*

ONCE THE PUBLIC memorial was over, George Richey could be found in the office at the house on Franklin Road, talking on the phone about how he was going to be able to turn the name "Tammy Wynette" into millions.

I tried very hard to give Richey the benefit of the doubt, hoping that I was wrong to feel that his histrionics were nothing more than a performance. I tried to be nice and ask few questions. I believed I should wait until the dust settled before I asked about the will or those yellow legal pads that contained Mom's instructions.

I don't want this to be a replay of Jackie's book. She details all of what happened with the will and the mysterious life insurance policy that was to go to the children but ended up going into the estate Richey controlled. But I will say this: nothing we had been told by Mom came about.

Richey took charge of everything, right down to our baby books. Not long after the money part began to play out, I remember saying to myself: *He's a scam artist. That's what this has all been about. He has spent years perfecting his con, and his fleecing of Tammy Wynette and her leg-*

acy is his masterpiece. During this time, Richey followed through on one bit of instruction that Mom had given him. For years, she had been asking him to put up iron gates at the front of the house on Franklin Road, and now he finally got around to doing it. Once they were in place, we were often turned away.

I hadn't planned on saying all this. In fact, because this book is about my mom and dad, I had intended to leave most of my thoughts about George Richey out of it. I had decided that because he was old and sick, I should just let it all go. But this summer, in July of 2010, something happened that changed everything. Richey died. And so I decided that I would go back and talk about him with complete openness. Sometimes honesty is not pretty.

Richey bought a BMW within weeks of Mom's death. Friends in Nashville began calling to tell me that he was seen at one event or another escorting a young woman named Sheila Slaughter, a former Dallas Cowboys cheerleader, around town. Sheila had met Mom while trying to break into the television production profession. She put together a show about Tanya Tucker and another about Mom. Sheila also helped Mom plan a baby shower for Faith Hill, which ended up costing a pile of money, expenses all okayed by Richey. Of course, Mom loved Faith, so anything that was done on her behalf would have been fine with her. But several people told me that the shower seemed to be in the hands of Sheila and Richey—not Sheila and Mom.

During the last year of Mom's life, Sheila was often seen at the Franklin Road house. Once Mom died, Sheila could be seen wearing her clothes and driving her cars. There was never a question in my mind as to why those iron gates went up at the Franklin Road house after Mom's funeral. Richey didn't want us to walk in on him and Sheila.

We were soon being shut out of as many events involving Mom as Richey could control. For example, not long after her death, the Eye, Ear, Nose, Throat Foundation put together a fund-raiser with various artists singing Mom's songs. The foundation approached us, and my sisters and I were happy to be invited. Then, seemingly out of nowhere, came an objection. Richey wanted our participation to be minimal, possibly even nonexistent. The foundation told him in no uncertain terms that they would not play those kinds of games. The foundation representative said that Tammy's daughters had been invited as honored guests and would remain so.

But we understood just how tricky things would be from then on. We were instructed to come directly to the ticket office to get our passes. What that proved to me was that Richey was still trying to control with an iron fist. If Mom's own children got in his way, then he planned on getting them completely out of the picture.

You want to know my actual thoughts? I walked into the ballroom and stood there looking at George Richey in a studded Versace jacket, thinking that he looked just like a pimp. A trashy pimp, dressed in expensive threads. That's exactly what I thought. And then there was his "date"—Sheila Slaughter, dressed in a low-cut gown, dress split up the side to her butt, and carrying a feather boa.

Oh yes—Tammy Wynette would have just loved that.

I was furious but determined to show no emotion or even to react just in case paparazzi were around to record the moment. But right then I saw Tina marching across the floor toward the couple.

Oh shit, I said to myself. *We are fixin' to be spread across every paper in the country.*

I rushed over and stopped her. "We can't make a scene, Tina," I reasoned.

Tina agreed. "I'm not going to make a scene, Georgette. I'm going to be very calm."

And so she continued. She walked over and confronted Sheila, asking her how she lived with herself knowing that Richey had killed Mom. And of course she meant that in the broadest terms—that whatever happened, he had worked Mom to death, allowed her to keep taking strong drugs, and that he even administered them himself. Tina wasn't even accusing him of intentionally murdering Mom. She was accusing him of sheer neglect of a very sick wife.

When Tina called Sheila a gold digger, Richey stepped in and tried to have a say. Tina told him off, too. I just stood there holding my breath and hoping that no punches were thrown! Tina ended up walking off. I was surprised, to tell the truth. The Tina I know has never been quite so low-key! (I was proud of my usually hotheaded sister.) When the story got written up in the tabloids, it somehow got expanded into a loud altercation in a stairwell and then was used by Richey to show that we daughters were a disrespectful lot.

My sisters and I filed a well-publicized lawsuit. We wanted an investigation of Mom's death. We wanted to know the answers to *so many* questions. Getting an autopsy was just the tip of the iceberg as far as we were concerned. I, for one, wanted to know just how many drugs had been coming to the house—what exactly had been injected into Mom? And by whom? Richey had appeared to be in a drug-induced state the day after Mom died. Was he drugged up when he was giving Mom medication? Why was 911 never called? Why was an out-of-town doctor called in to pronounce Mom dead? Why had a large order of Dilaudid been delivered to the house on Franklin Road? She wasn't supposed to be taking that drug! There were just too many questions.

It took a great deal of perseverance, but we finally forced Richey into the position of having to ask for an autopsy. He announced that he was having it performed and that it was a case of Tammy's daughters doing their mother's memory a disservice. No. It was a case of her daughters taking a stand she could no longer take.

The autopsy didn't tell much, however. For example, they found that she had painkillers including Versed and Phenergan in her system, but there was no way to tell if there was any Dilaudid. The bottom line? There was no real way to say precisely how she died. But we had tried. The famed medical examiner Cyril Wecht looked at the case and said much could have been solved if a complete accounting of how much medication Mom had been given that day had been available on the day she died. Personally, I believe that what killed her was an overdose of Versed. It's a dangerous drug that should never be administered by an amateur like Richey.

Meanwhile, we received word that Mom's credit cards were being used to buy women's clothing in Dallas, just three days following her death.

We were given $5,000 apiece as sort of a consolation prize, I guess. Something to keep us pacified for the time being. Tina refused it; she knew it was a bogus offering. At that point, we all should have known that a charade was being played out. Mom's original will never showed up. The insurance policies were not what we had been told they would be. And according to Richey, everything would now go toward promoting Mom's name. How that would happen would be up to him. Richey didn't even follow through on keeping fresh flowers coming to Mom's grave.

Tina, Jackie, and I gave up even trying to be nice to Richey. We'd played his game for months, hoping at least to get access to our baby books and a few personal items that were in the house. But it was not to be, so we turned our backs on him. Gwen tried to stay above the fray, keeping an open mind and hoping we were all wrong.

MY FATHER WATCHED all this go down with great disgust. Dad has been around enough phonies to know one in a heartbeat. He knew we were probably fighting a no-win battle for any part of Mom's estate. The fix was in even before she died.

Mom never wanted it to end this way. She had wanted her children taken care of, and she'd worked hard to see that it happened. And when I say children, I include George Richey's children. She had attempted to make provisions for them as well.

It is almost like a bad dream to go back over those months following Mom's death. In addition to being locked out of Mom's world and kept away from my own belongings there on Franklin Road, I saw that Richey had taken final control over Mom—that she hadn't escaped even in death.

One thing that Dad and Nancy tried to do was to see that Mom had a burial place befitting her stature in the country music world. Richey had at least listened to us when we insisted she be buried aboveground, but aboveground was as far as it went. Mom was put in an unremarkable vault at Woodlawn. There is nothing special, no real place for fans to gather to pay tribute to her. After she had been exhumed for the autopsy, Dad and Nancy talked to us about putting her in a distinctive mausoleum, one befitting the First Lady of Country Music.

The cost for doing that would run about $25,000. That was more than Richey wanted to spend, and so Dad and Nancy came up with another idea. They purchased a large plot where several country stars and their spouses could be buried—including Dad and Nancy.

Dad had already been in charge of his friend Johnny Paycheck's burial. It broke Dad's heart when he learned that Johnny had passed away and that Johnny's widow not only didn't have the money to bury him, she didn't even have money to buy him a new suit! Dad was just sick that he hadn't known Johnny was in that kind of a situation. He was a star who made a lot of money for managers, promoters, record labels—all kinds of people. And there wasn't even enough money to buy him a new suit. Of course Dad stepped in, his only regret being that he hadn't helped sooner.

The final site for Tammy Wynette, First Lady of Country Music, would include a spot for her husband, George Richey. No one tried to ease him out of the picture. Nancy even wanted to know if any of us girls wanted to be buried there, so she would make sure they had the space to do it. You've got to hand it to this woman—trying to make sure her husband's former wife had a fine burial spot. When it was clear that Richey didn't want to spend any money, Nancy suggested we raise the money. "Do it," Richey said.

This time Gwen ended it. In her mind, Mom had been disturbed once, for the autopsy, and so she should be left alone. She also didn't like the idea that Mom would be interred in what she thought might be a kind of country music "theme cemetery." I hope she rethinks her position one day, because Mom deserves a better burial site than what she now has. I still hope that Mom gets the kind of final resting spot she deserves, something suitable for country royalty. And I know that as long as my dad and Nancy live, they will make sure that it is done with taste and respect.

But I couldn't help but wonder what I'd feel like if I one day stood at my father's grave site and hadn't made the effort to really get to know this man. I made up my mind that I would not allow that to happen.

TWENTY-FIVE

JUST WHEN YOU THINK THINGS can't get any worse—they do.

Throughout the days following Mom's death, I had my own drama playing out. Actually, there were several of them. For one thing, I still had to go to court on that assault charge. My attorney had told me not to worry about it, that it would most likely be thrown out of court, but I felt snakebit. I had no idea what would happen. On top of that, I was just coming to a final agreement with Joel about custody of our sons. I was depressed. At one point, I had been suicidal.

Then, fate must have decided to smack me one final time. An old health issue popped back up in a very ugly form.

In 1992, before Joel and I got married, I had a Pap smear that showed some precancerous cells. I had a procedure called cryosurgery, which freezes the bad cells and then sloughs them off. It's a simple procedure, and used for all kinds of things, from warts and moles to various cancers. Not usually a big deal, because many women have these precancerous cells and are treated successfully.

Joel and I married that June, and I never gave the next testing time much thought with all the excitement of the wedding. But my next checkup showed that the precancerous cells had spread. The next thing we tried was called a conization, or a cone biopsy. This time the results came up normal after three months, in June of '92. But the very day of the tests was when I experienced some pain and learned that I was having an ectopic pregnancy. I had emergency surgery, and we thought everything was fine—especially after I gave birth to healthy twin boys the following year.

I didn't just forget about the condition, though. I was careful to have my Pap smear testing over the years. Despite all that was going on, I was vigilant about the tests, and sure enough, in September of 1998, the test showed cancerous cells on my cervix. With my history, the doctors recommended a hysterectomy.

I was devastated. Lying there in the hospital after having the hysterectomy, I felt like someone had stolen my "womanhood." I know that sounds silly in a way, because no one thing makes up a woman's "femaleness." And I understood that I had to take precautions against this cancer growing and ultimately taking my life.

I had always wanted more children. I was one of those

people who envisioned herself with a house full of children, running and playing. I was torn up with conflicts! At the very time I was saddened at the thought of having no chance to give birth again, I was filled with happiness that I did have my sons. My boys were four years old, healthy and happy.

And so when I sorted it all out, I had to consider the whole picture. I wasn't married, and I had actually come to a time when I was questioning that I wanted to be tied to a man anyway. I knew that I couldn't take any chances that might shorten my life. No matter what, I had to be there for my twins.

I remember thinking how badly I wanted my mother with me during that time. I wanted to talk to Mom, to hear her telling me that I was doing the right thing. Of course I knew that's what she would say. But I still wanted to hear her say it. I knew then that I was facing years ahead when I'd need her advice about child rearing and she wouldn't be there.

But despite the feeling that fate was messing with me, I sometimes wonder if Mom was smiling down on me. Things did work out. The surgery was a success. Joel and I came to a good agreement about shared custody. No matter what our personal problems were, Joel always loved our sons and put them first. He is a good father and is now married to a wonderful woman who treats the boys as though they were her own. I don't mean she wants to take my place, but she wants them to know how they are loved and welcome in their father's home. I thank the Lord for that.

And my court case ended up just like the attorney predicted: the policewoman's accusations were thrown out. She wanted to charge me with assault that resulted in a permanent injury, but that presented just a small problem: she had tried the same trick regarding the same "injury" before!

MOM STAYED ON my mind a lot that year. My Lord, I missed her. I couldn't help but think about her last weeks and wonder what they were like. I wondered if she really knew what she meant to me—to all of her daughters. Mother's Day of 1999 was coming up. It had been about a year since Mom's death. I was still thinking about those final weeks, wondering if she knew just how much she was loved.

I found that I was angry a lot of the time. I was mad at Richey for having treated Mom badly, and mad at the coroner and the media and anyone else who didn't seem to want to know exactly what had happened to her on the last day. I was especially mad that there were some who believed Mom's daughters were only asking questions because they wanted money. Of course we wanted Mom's estate to be settled fairly, the way she told us it would be done. And of course we believed we were due part of it. But it was less about what was happening to Mom's money than about what had happened to Mom's instructions.

I kept thinking about the times we found out that she had been in the hospital—those times were almost never because of George Richey's doings. He seldom informed us about what was going on. But—and I have been told this by many people, including Mom—he would then comment to her: "I just can't imagine why those girls haven't called or come to see you."

I could have told him why. We were not told what was going on.

Yes, I stayed mad. And uninterrupted anger is not a good place to be, especially for someone who just survived cervical cancer. The anger wasn't just over how my sisters and I were perceived, though. I thought so many times about how Richey treated Mom and wondered if it was even worse than I had believed.

It broke my heart every time I thought about the things she said that Richey had told her. He had threatened to "expose" her as a drug addict, and (in his words, according to Mom) a "whore." That's how he kept her in line. Why, oh why did she not just leave, go to one of her friends, like Jan Howard or Loretta Lynn? Why didn't she come to one of her daughters? I thought long and hard about the fact that Mom seemed to require a man around at all times, even when that man was destructive to her.

I decided that I was going to stop that cycle in my own life. I made a vow to stop believing that I had to have a boyfriend who either lived with me or who wanted me to live with him. I wanted to learn to be happy simply being a mom to my boys, happy doing my job at the hospital, and satisfied with my life as it unfolded.

Mom's death and having that cancer so close together changed me. I realized that happiness is too often fleeting in life, and that you should appreciate the times you are truly content. Losing Mom made me appreciate Dad so much more—I prayed for a relationship with him. And, I might add, I thanked God that he had found Nancy. Oh, how I wished Mom had found someone with Nancy's personality.

And I prayed that Mom knew how much I loved her.

As Mother's Day grew closer in 1999, I started writing down a few thoughts. I didn't start out by thinking in terms of writing a song. I was just putting words on paper. But being from a musical family, those words began to come out as lyrics. They became a way of me talking to Mom, of expressing my feelings instead of holding things in until they exploded.

One of the most important things I wanted her to know was that I still felt like her little girl. I could hear her humming songs to me, could feel her arms around me. I could hear her telling me how much she loved me.

I wanted Mom to know that the love she had for me would live always in my heart.

I thought about the times as a teenager when I insisted on having things go my way—like when I didn't want to come back to Nashville with Mom and Richey. I hoped she knew that it wasn't because I loved her any less, I just wanted to finish school with my friends. I wonder why I never really explained it better to her, why I hadn't explained myself every step of the way.

I Hope You Knew

I remember sitting in your lap. You would hum
in my ear.
I still feel your arms around me. They were warm
and erased all my fear.
I was your little baby girl, you said I took your
breath away.
And the love you gave so completely, I carry in
my heart today.

Now I wish that I could tell you all the things you said were true.
I want to thank you for your love and the little things you used to do.

I know God took you for a reason, and I'm sure Heaven welcomed you.
I still want to say I love you, but I can't.

I hope you knew.

My teenage years took their toll, but you loved me anyway.
I guess I took it all for granted that moms were supposed to be that way.
Now I'm finally all grown up with two children of my own.
And so many things I would have asked you if only I had known.
Now I wish that I could tell you all the things you said were true.
I want to thank you for your love and the little things you used to do. I know God took you for a reason, and I know Heaven welcomed you.

I still want to say I love you, but I can't. I hope you knew.
I still want to say I love you, but I can't.

I hope you knew.

It was important for me to write that song. It told me that I had important things to say and that I could communicate in simple, heartfelt lyrics. And it played into another change that was taking place. I had started to conclude that I needed to get better at communication. When I'd clammed up to Mom about the problems in my first marriage, I had alienated her for months! I hadn't been honest with Dad about how much I wanted to be close to him. And, of course, I hadn't put my foot down about some issues I had with George Richey and Mom. I don't know if my saying anything would have made a difference, but I wished I'd tried harder. The one chance I had to be honest was in my relationship with Dad. I started by asking his advice about the lyrics I wrote for "I Hope You Knew." Now I had to take it a step further.

Over a year had passed since Mom died. My heart was breaking that she was not going to be around to see my boys, Kyle and Ryan, grow up. They were developing into such distinct personalities, too! I've always heard that by the time a child is around six years old, much of the personality is formed. That certainly proved true with my twins. They still have those personalities they had back when they were younger.

Kyle is my social butterfly, Mr. Popular. He knows everybody, loves to visit with people, to play sports and meet new people. He's very organized and responsible. In fact, sometimes even as a child he tried to act as if he were the parent! I sometimes had to remind him that *I* was the mom and *he* was the child! Kyle studies hard and makes good grades—he always has. I never have to worry about him getting homework done or forgetting his chores.

Ryan is more introverted. He's a quiet boy with a heart of gold. He's full of energy, and on the go, but if you want his opinion, you'll have to ask him for it. He loves computers, tinkering with things, and anything mechanical. He has good friends, but unlike his brother, he's not on the phone planning things or wanting to go places all the time. Kyle is the one who's always off with pals, and Ryan is more likely to be home with me, working on his computer or building something. Both of them are the great joys of my life.

Even when they were young, those two personalities were so evident, so wonderful, that I was determined that they would get to know my dad. I wanted them to have him in their lives, and I wanted *him* to have *them*!

I called and told Dad that I was going to bring the boys for a visit, and asked what would be a good time to come by his house. I thought we had it all settled. Until I showed up at the main gate and rang the house. No one answered. I stood out there for a long time, but it appeared that no one was home. I got out my cell phone and dialed Nancy. Again, there was no answer. I left a message, then got back in the car, stammered some excuse to the boys, and left. Then, just as I turned onto I-65 to head back to Alabama, I caught a glimpse of Dad and Nancy driving toward the house.

I had two reactions. First, I almost cried. I was sure that they had avoided us, that they had ignored the phone call I'd made and tried to stay away until we left. *Why?* I just couldn't understand it. Why did Dad do this kind of thing? After the kindness he'd shown during the days just after Mom's death, how could he treat my boys and me like this? Then I got pissed off. And I stayed pissed off.

Suddenly, about halfway back to Alabama, my cell phone rang. It was Nancy calling to apologize for missing us. I told her we were pulling into a truck stop and I would call her right back. I told the boys I needed to make a call. I stood in the parking lot of the truck stop, where I could see the boys, but they couldn't hear me. I called her back, and asked her if she had a few minutes to listen to something I had to say.

"Of course I do," Nancy said.

I just let it rip.

"All I want is an honest answer," I said. "Does Dad want me and my boys in his life?"

I told her that I had spent my whole life trying to have a relationship with my father, and every time I opened myself up, I felt like I'd been rejected.

"I'm gonna tell you the truth, Nancy," I said. "I've got used to being rejected. It's normal for me. But I am not gonna have my boys think it's normal. Kyle and Ryan don't deserve this."

I explained that I was not going to start making up excuses for him, either. I was not going to start telling the boys that their grandfather was called away at the last minute. I wasn't going to invent some lie when all it was really about was that he didn't want to see us.

"It'll be easier to just tell them right now that it's not gonna happen—that they are not gonna have a relationship with their granddad. Why pretend?"

I was just getting wound up when Nancy stopped me.

The first thing she told me was that the mix-up on that day was a real mix-up, not some plot instigated by Dad against the boys and me. *But,* she explained, he was sometimes apprehensive when he knew I planned on coming. He wasn't always sure what we'd talk about or if we had much in common despite our recent reconciliation. I had to admit that I sometimes wondered about the reconciliation as well. Was it simply something that happened in the wake of a tragedy and was then meaningless?

"I need you to understand something about your father, Georgette," she said. "You need to understand about the walls he has built around him."

Then she talked very honestly with me about the times Dad's business associates, friends, and even his family had been a source of pain. And she said he didn't trust most people, not deep down. This was not the first time I'd been told most of these stories. She had tried to explain it to me before. But this time she really got through *and* she had an idea.

Nancy's idea was this: let's not warn him anyone is coming. That way he won't worry about it. Let's just have his daughter and grandsons show up. Then, over time, the fear of being hurt or used will lessen.

And that's exactly what we did. Oh, Nancy knew we were coming. Sometimes she told Dad and sometimes she didn't. And a funny thing started happening. Dad started enjoying our visits. He loved the boys, and they loved him. They had no ulterior motives. They didn't want a thing from him, not presents, or money, or any special help. They just wanted to have a granddad.

For me these visits took on a strange tone. This is going to sound bizarre, but in some ways, I felt like I was on a blind date! I asked all sorts of questions about how Dad felt about this and that, if he'd ever been to this city or that city, what kinds of movies he liked. It was as if we were getting to know each other for the first time.

And we started looking forward to our talks. Dad liked knowing more about me, and I was thrilled to have access to my father finally. The silly thing is that the things we talked about back then were boring in a way—the kinds of things that people know about each other when they are family.

Best of all, Dad became the kind of grandfather that Kyle and Ryan dreamed of having. He loved spending time with them, talking, listening to the stories about their world. He got a kick out of Ryan's love of tearing things apart and "fixing" them. Dad called him "the screwdriver." He loved Kyle's outgoing, easy personality. And he noticed that they seemed to love music.

That's how we operated for the next several years. It took that long for me to feel comfortable with Dad. I had never known, for example, when Dad was joking and when he wasn't. Let me tell you, you can get your feelings hurt if you don't know when someone is kidding around! And my dad has a dry wit—it's easy to mistake one of his jokes for something serious.

I still use Nancy as my sounding board. If I have news to spring on Dad, I ask her if the time is right. If I need his help with something, I run it by her.

I learned that it was okay for me to ask him questions about our family—about the Jones family. I wanted to know so much, and I'd never asked him questions in my entire life. Being able to talk to him about family matters made me all the sadder that I didn't have Mom to question. Oh, how I wish I'd asked her about her side of the family. Of course,

I knew more about them because of MeeMaw and PeePaw, but I still have things I'd love to talk with her about.

I thought a great deal about Dad, and about how I felt about what had happened between us. It's probably hard for people to understand if they had a very close, personal relationship with both of their parents from the time they were born. But for those of us who somehow lost the connection or never had it in the first place, there is nothing more wonderful than taking those baby steps to love and trust. I wrote down some thoughts, and then I approached two writer friends, Don Pfrimmer and Mark McGuinn.

What came together was my heart put down on paper.

Dad and I recorded "You and Me and Time," and I began to think about what I had missed by not having more music in my life. It occurred to me that time was bringing me back to my father, and to music.

YOU AND ME AND TIME

You were just a picture on my baby grand.
Yours was in my wallet I showed to all my friends.
But the world rolled in between us, keeping us apart.
Thank God, we discovered we're still joined at the heart.

You and me and time finally got together.
I'm sorry that it took so long, but better late than never.
The love we thought we'd lost was not that hard to find.
It only took the three of us, you and me and time.

I lost you to the spotlight but kept you in my prayers.
No matter where it took me, hun, you were always
there.
It's so hard when your hero is a stranger in your home.
Our love is like a mountain. One can't move it alone.

We can't light the candles on the birthdays that
we missed,
But we can hold each other and thank the Lord
for this . . .

Daddy, you and me and time finally got together.
I'm sorry that it took so long, but better late than
never.
The love we thought we'd lost was not that hard to
find.
It only took the three of us, you and me and time.
It only took the three of us, you and me and time.

TWENTY-SIX

I HAD BACKED AWAY FROM performing music for years, terrified that people would expect another Tammy Wynette or George Jones, afraid I'd fall short by comparison. My fears were so strong that I hadn't even tried, much less failed.

Then, in late 1998, when Mom had been dead about six months, I had an invitation to participate in a project called Country Family Reunions, performing with second-generation artists including Ronnie Robbins (son of Marty), Robin Young (son of Faron), Hawkshaw Hawkins Jr. (son of Hawkshaw), Jett Williams (daughter of Hank), Michael Twitty (son of Conway), and Dean Miller (son of Roger). The performances of the "star children" were to be videotaped, along with those of some

Opry greats, resulting in songs known and loved through country music's history.

I agreed to do it but was scared to death. I hadn't performed in years, and I knew that many of the participants were doing stage shows, writing, and performing—they were professionals. I felt like a complete amateur.

I'm not even sure if I would have had the courage to sing at all if not for Mom's close friend Jan Howard. My embarrassment over being so out of practice was compounded by the fact that I had misunderstood what was expected of me. The problem, apparently, was because the woman I spoke with didn't know what segment of the series I was to participate in. As it turned out, I was to sing *two* of my parents' songs, but had only prepared "Apartment Number Nine." I chose that because both parents had recorded it. It could have been a disaster, but Jan Howard saved the day and performed "Your Good Girl's Gonna Go Bad" with me. Everyone was wonderful. Bill Anderson hosted the show, with Opry stars like Jan, Skeeter Davis, and Jim Ed Brown.

After the filming, most of the other second-generation singers met in downtown Nashville for a drink. It was the first time in years that I had been around people I'd known as a child and who had many of the same early experiences as I did. They understood what it was like to travel with a parent, to check tour schedules to know where your mom or dad is going to be at some particular time, and sometimes to learn what a parent was doing by seeing it on a tabloid cover!

We also shared some frustrations about music, about the commonly held belief that "stardom" should have come easy for stars' children, and yet never did. All of us knew what it meant to be compared to a famous parent. And with me, it was about two famous parents.

That day was important to me. I loved the camaraderie, the mutual understanding, the performing—and the music. And for the first time I knew that others felt exactly as I did! I wasn't the only insecure child of a star. I didn't immediately decide to try my hand at the family business, but it definitely started a flame burning inside of me. I started thinking back to the time I had spent singing on the road with Mom during the '70s and '80s. I even thought about times I'd been onstage with both my parents. And I wished we'd done more singing together.

I thought about making a demo tape for the next year or so. A lot of people who heard me sing on Country Family Reunions started encouraging me, friends talked to me, and finally, after I had written the words about how I felt about Mom, I decided to take action.

It took every bit of courage I had, but I approached Dad for advice:

"Dad, I wrote some words that I hope can become a song. Can you help me find someone to work with on them, someone to help me make a demo?"

I didn't know what he might say when he started reading what I'd written, the lyrics to "I Hope You Knew."

I think if he had only had a lukewarm response, I would never have started on this career path. I believe that I would have finished my song for Mom, and that would have been the end of it. But Dad not only took my lyrics seriously, he loved the song and wanted to help. He told me I should approach a fellow named Ernie Rowell who would be good at working on the melody and on producing some demo tapes for me.

Later, Dad got even more involved when he asked me to open for him at a 2002 show in Nashville's historic Ryman Auditorium. The Ryman is where the Grand Ole Opry became the biggest show in country music, and stepping onto that stage has been the goal of performers for decades. It was on an old flatbed truck in front of the Ryman that Mom had first performed a song for a Nashville audience. It didn't matter to her whether the tourists were just milling around and that she was just another hopeful. She was *there*. I thought about the times that Dad and Mom stepped on that stage and made country music history with songs like "Stand by Your Man" and "He Stopped Loving Her Today." And when I walked up to sing next to my father, I thought of my parents standing there singing their great duet hits like "Golden Ring." I felt so close to Mom as I stood there beside Dad.

Being on the same bill with him reminded me of the last time I ever saw my parents sing together. It was at a concert in Birmingham, Alabama, in 1997, just a year before Mom died. Both events brought tears to my eyes.

Ernie did help me with the song, but it took me until 2003 to decide to make a three-song demo. Those three songs quickly became five, then seven and eight—until I had twelve songs on tape! It took every cent I could put together.

I learned a great deal on this project. I hired the best musicians I could find, and went out in Nashville looking for songs. But ultimately, while I had some good songs, there were not enough of the best compositions Nashville had to offer. Publishers don't give their best songs to people just starting out—even if the people wanting the songs are related to country music royalty. And they especially don't give their best songs to female vocalists over the age of thirty! What I learned was this: I needed to write more songs myself, and I needed to meet more of Nashville's songwriting community. Nevertheless, I pitched my project to every label in town, large and small.

I was offered several deals with small record labels. One was even willing to pay me a $30,000 signing fee. But it would have tied me up for three years and had some other drawbacks in the contract. Still another label offered what appeared to be a fantastic deal. But that company turned out to be a sham, and it suddenly closed. It was clear that I needed some business help on this journey!

That help showed up when I met Jackie Bradshaw and Jim Foster, from Cosmic Mule Music. They turned out to be just what I needed. And so, as I learned to deal with losing Mom and with trying to reestablish ties with Dad, I was drawn back into music. But I think it is important to know that I came back to performing *through* writing—through putting my emotions down on paper. That's why finding a good publishing company, one that would help me meet and work with other writers, was so important.

I signed with Cosmic Mule in 2005, and in the process, met and signed with Nashville attorney Philip Lyon. *That* was the smartest thing I have ever done! You have *no idea* how many bad deals are waiting for every hopeful in the music business. The music sharks are everywhere, and unless you can instinctively spot them, you better have some savvy people on your team. Philip led my team, which included Cosmic Mule Music, and they kept me from making a lot of mistakes.

That same year, I attended Country Radio Seminar (CRS) in Nashville. I made a new demo tape, produced by Jim Foster, featuring my own material, and passed it around at CRS. I was thrilled to get good reviews from two of Nashville's top writers, Robert K. Oermann and Phil Sweetland. That positive response gave me more hope than I can explain, because I knew that "who" I was didn't have anything to do with it. In fact, I almost believe I got great reviews in spite of my name!

In 2005, RCA decided to give another listen to that demo tape Jim had produced. After they listened again, they asked Jim to have me come to Nashville and sing for them in person. I jumped at the chance. I was still living in Alabama and working as a nurse. So every time I went back and forth, I had to juggle the boys, the job, and the money it took to get back to Tennessee. As I started getting serious about the music, I often thought about times Mom had said that she hated the fact that her career had taken her away from her daughters so much. I felt the same way. There was so much guilt when I'd have to leave and run to Nashville for a session or a meeting. But, I thought, maybe this one would be the payoff.

When RCA asked me to sing for them, I was so excited that I found myself starting to dial Mom's phone number to tell her the good news.

I ended up singing three songs for Joe Galante, the head of RCA, and Renee Bell, the VP of A&R (artists and repertoire). I brought guitarist Scott Coney with me as an accompanist, and I did the songs. They loved a song I wrote titled "When Tractors Fly." Part of the song goes like this:

WHEN TRACTORS FLY

I found the road to travel is dusty dirt and gravel,
no concrete.
I love to walk for hours in ditches full of flowers
in bare feet.
When I was a city girl, I didn't realize
that a country boy could change the way I dream
of livin' life.

Now, I don't mind the rooster crowin',
fixin' fences, paintin' barns.
Sleepin' with my windows open,
so contented in your arms.

If I ever leave you, you can look up in the sky.
I'll be headed for the city . . . when tractors fly.

Just before Christmas of 2006, an RCA representative called to ask me if I would play a showcase for them. So in February of 2007, I played a show at Nashville's 12th & Porter. It started out feeling good. Joe Galante was there and had his photo taken with me. Tammy Genovese from the Country Music Association came to do a piece for the CMA's *Close Up* magazine. I didn't actually see Renee Bell there, but others did, so I knew she'd attended. That did make me a little nervous—the fact that she hadn't approached me to say hello or comment on the show. Still, I knew that people at the label had said they loved my demo, so in my heart I believed that I had the record deal.

A FEW DAYS later Philip Lyon received a text message from Renee. RCA was passing. The label did not feel that I was a "different" enough artist.

I was devastated. For the next several months, I could not sing or write. It was too painful. Finally, I had to sit down and remind myself that I was not following this path for recognition or a pat on the head. I was doing it in hopes of making a career change or being able to work in a direction I had come to love. I'd fought against trying to follow a music dream for so many years that, once on that road, I'd allowed myself to hope for too much, too soon.

What I needed to keep in mind was that I was looking for a *way* to make this my career. That meant I had to find opportunities to *earn a living* in music. With Philip's help, I began making some wise career moves, to book shows and personal appearances. I recorded a duet with Mark McGuinn that was included on his CD *One Man's Crazy.* I filmed the Del Shores television series *Sordid Lives,* with Emmy-winning actor Leslie Jordan, Bonnie Bedelia, Olivia Newton-John, and Margaret Cho. I also recorded three of Mom's songs for the sound track of the series. Those sessions gave me the incredible opportunity to work with the legendary Los Angeles producer Michael Lloyd.

Then, my father came through for me once again—just when I needed a boost. Dad offered to record "You and Me and Time" with me and helped get some publicity for our song. He released the song as the first single from his

CD *Burn Your Playhouse Down*. He had his public relations agent, Kirt Webster, set up a lot of press for us, and that is *not* something Dad relishes doing! But the moment I almost came to tears was when, at Country Radio Seminar, Dad talked to the deejays about "You and Me and Time," asking them to play the song. He explained that he wasn't asking on his own behalf, but because it was a song he'd done with his daughter and it would mean a lot to him for it to be played on the radio. And while it wasn't one of the year's biggest hits, I know that it got a lot of airplay because of Dad's request.

In 2009, the chance came to play a series of shows in Ireland. At that point, I had to make a choice: quit my nursing job and pursue music full-time or continue to play it safe. I chose to throw caution to the wind.

(Of course, like Mom did with her beautician certification, I will never let my nursing credentials run out!)

The trip brought more to my life than I ever dreamed. Our first venue that July was in Donegal, Ireland. I briefly talked with the steel player, Jamie Lennon, who told me he was planning on moving to Nashville to pursue his music. In a way it reminded me of what I had done—changed my life to follow a dream. I talked with him every so often through the next few shows, but it was always very formal and polite. I thought he was a really nice guy but never thought in terms of seeing him personally. (I hadn't dated in a long time, trying to break that pattern of "always needing a man.")

Things changed one afternoon when I was with Philomena Begley, the great Queen of Irish Country Music, waiting for Hal Ketchum to finish his sound check prior to a show at the Knightsbrook Hotel.

Philomena, who is an irrepressibly funny woman, decided that Jamie Lennon and I made a good match, and she wasn't satisfied until we were sitting together, talking, and getting to know each other. The Queen of Irish Country Music was right. We did make a good match, and by the time I went back to the States just a few weeks later, we were inseparable. I loved the serious way he approached his music, his sense of humor, and his honesty. We spent hours on the telephone, on Skype, and by the time Jamie came to the States, it felt like we'd known each other for decades. The more I knew about Jamie, the more I respected him. For one thing, he also had children from a first marriage that he loved very much. As we spoke more and more about our feelings on parenting, I saw we had many shared goals and convictions.

As time went by, I realized what I had been missing in my relationships. I didn't need to marry because it was the thing to do, or because we were living together anyway, or because I needed someone to take care of me. I needed and wanted a partner, someone who cared about my goals and wanted to help me achieve them, someone whose goals and aspirations I cared about and supported.

When Jamie proposed marriage in October of 2009, I happily accepted.

The one question I had was how to tell Dad. He had always been watchful about men I dated, and I didn't know if he would think Jamie and I had enough time together to make the decision to marry.

It was funny to see Dad and Jamie interact at first. Dad's a little hard of hearing, and with Jamie's English accent, the two had some difficulty communicating. Then I started to see the two of them laugh at various stories when they talked, sharing stories about music and musicianship and favorite songs. And in the end, the two got along very well. Dad approved and grew to enjoy Jamie's company very much.

I've watched their relationship develop, and they are becoming good friends. That's saying something for Dad, because he doesn't let just anybody get close. Dad's very slow to hand out his approval, but once you have him on your side—he is there.

One of the things he loves to do is "introduce" Jamie to certain American delicacies. One time when the four of us were in Cracker Barrel, Dad passed a small bowl of grits to Jamie.

"You like grits, don't you, son?"

The look on Jamie's face was priceless. He didn't know what to say because he didn't want to hurt Dad's feelings. Then he saw the twinkle in Dad's eye and realized that it was a joke. That's what I meant earlier. Dad loves to joke and you don't always know when he's doing it! It's like that television show where people get "punked."

Jamie had been punked in Cracker Barrel.

We spent Thanksgiving of 2009 with Dad and Nancy, and I don't think I ever laughed any harder at my father. We had a lot of people at the house—so many that we were eating on paper plates with plastic knives and forks.

"Nancy, get Jamie a china plate and some real silverware," Dad suddenly announced. Then, while Nancy went to the kitchen, Dad explained.

"This is your first time at a family dinner, Jamie," Dad said. "And I think we should make it special. But don't count on this treatment all the time. From now on, you'll eat on paper plates like the rest of us!"

My boys adore Jamie. He's like a big kid playing with them, but he also understands the role of a parent and doesn't actually expect to "be" a kid. I think it's important to remember that. You can't forget your role in the family. I always considered Mom a friend, and she was fun—but I never forgot that she was the mom! Of course, things have changed so much as my boys have gone through their teen years. Society is different, more complex. There are more dangers for young people now, with influences like the Internet. But I believe my boys have come through like champs. It's hard to believe that they are seventeen this year, and so mature. I'm proud of them both.

In December of 2009, I had an offer from a record label—a small, independent label, but one that believed in me and was willing to take a chance. Tracy Pitcox at Heart of Texas told me to write some songs, find some songs, pick some songs from Mom and Dad's repertoire—in short, to make him an album that showed all the sides of my music, from history to the present day. I jumped at the chance. It was important to me to pay tribute to both my parents on the album, to give them the respect I believe they are due for my musical heritage. I no longer fear that people will compare us.

After much thought, I decided to put one of my favorite of Mom's self-penned songs on the album, as the title cut: "A Slightly Used Woman." I've always loved this song's haunting melody and the way that it described our first

Franklin Road home in Nashville, the one where I was a child. Also, as an adult I understood and related to the words in the song. And I understand that Mom felt that way—slightly used. I think a lot of people feel the same.

My dad worried some that my contract wasn't with a big label, one with a lot of money to give me for an advance and tour support. But Dad also started out on a small Texas label, and he knows I had the offer I wanted, from someone willing to show the past, present, and future of my music loves. One song I wrote for the project is titled "Leavin' Yesterday."

I had the title and the idea, and talked to a writer named Jeff Ross about working on it with me. I knew that there were times in my life that I should have done something "yesterday"—*should* have realized a relationship was wrong, *should* have given up on old hurts—*should have, should have!* So much music comes from misery. But maybe the best lessons come in songs about how one deals with bad times.

LEAVIN' YESTERDAY

I should stop makin' excuses, waitin' and hopin' you
are gonna magically change.
None of our problems are goin' away.
I should stop lookin' for answers and puttin' this off.
Tomorrow will still be the same.
I should be leavin' yesterday.

I should stop tryin' to fix you,
You're not really broken.
It's just not how I thought it would be.

You've done all you can do,
I've said all I can say,
I should stop fightin' and cryin',
and finding fault in you
when I should just be findin' my keys.
I should be leavin' yesterday.

Yesterday I could have left this baggage at our front door,
Yesterday I could have hated you, just a little bit more.

Can't you just make this easy,
stop makin' me love you.
Don't stand there lookin' at me that way.
Hell, I should be leavin' yesterday.
Yeah, I should be leavin' yesterday.

And so, right after Christmas of 2009, I recorded the project with producer Justin Trevino, in Texas. My fiancé, Jamie, played steel on everything except, of course, "You and Me and Time," which I'd recorded before I met Jamie. What a wonderful feeling—to work on songs I love with the man I love!

We plan on making another album for Heart of Texas in early 2011. And yes, I will include some songs from both my mom and my dad. It is very important to me to continue to show those sides of my persona and my music.

I know that I am never going to have the career that either of my parents had. I will not be another "next big thing" like Taylor Swift or Carrie Underwood. I started following my dream too late for that sort of a career. But this is my career—and I believe my mom would approve of me doing it just the way I have. I had to see the direction before I could go after the goal.

If I have learned anything through the last decade or so, it is this: take nothing for granted. Don't take your parents for granted, because you can wake up one morning and one of them can be gone at a young age. I wish now that I had made every day I had with Mom count more than I did. But what I learned from her death went on to help me know that it is never too late to change. It was not too late for me to have a good relationship with my father. As the song said, it took both of us and *time*—but we did it.

Family is what life is about. I need my sons, my father—and now Jamie, the man I will marry in 2011. Those are the meaningful things, not careers or money in the bank. I guess you could say that through some very sad times, I learned to allow myself to be happy. I gave myself permission to enjoy life and truly love the people in mine. You shouldn't get into the habit of regretting what you've done in life. I've stopped regretting things I've done, stopped calling them mistakes or crying over a misstep.

Let's face it: if I hadn't married my first husband, I would not have gone to Alabama, where I met and married Joel Smith, the father of my two wonderful sons, Kyle and Ryan. If I hadn't decided years later to stop looking for love, and to pursue my career path alone, I would not have met Jamie Lennon.

This career I'm working on does leave me with a lot of guilt. I'd always had a stable job and been home for the boys. And even though they are now seventeen years old, I worry about not being there for every one of their events—large and small. My understanding of Mom has become so much more complete. We were her life, but so was music. It became a balancing act.

I've tried to be more communicative with the boys than my parents were with me. I've learned that even when you think you are doing them a favor by hiding things, you seldom are. That doesn't mean they have to be a part of every decision. The twins' father, Joel Smith, and I have tried hard to work out our problems without dragging them into it. Joel even brags to the boys about their grandmother's cooking. I had to smile one day when I overheard him telling them how much he loved her amazing breakfasts, with biscuits and gravy, pork chops, eggs, and potatoes. Let someone else tell them about her music—family should remember Tammy Wynette's biscuits!

Communication is crucial to almost everything in life. If, like me, you find it difficult, I suggest you start out changing by writing down your feelings. If you are musical, the thoughts may come out as lyrics. They may be poetry. Or you may write down how you feel in a letter or journal. Then, hopefully, you will take the next step, and speak those thoughts.

As I move on to another phase of my life, I think back on life thus far. And when I think of my mother, I will think of the funny woman wearing sunglasses and a ponytail, whisking me into some carnival fun house, saying, "Don't be scared, Georgette." I'll think of Mom on the tour bus cooking ham and dumplin's for the band. I'll think of Dad standing there in the foyer in Mom's home, knowing how much I needed him on the day of her death. And when I think of my dad, I'll start by remembering Mom's story about him jumping up in the air and clicking his heels on the day I was born.

"Hot a'mighty!"

ACKNOWLEDGMENTS

I WANT TO START BY thanking Nancy Jones for her love and unwavering commitment in helping Dad and me mend our relationship. Thank you, Nancy, for believing in me and my music, and for being there for me as a mother would be. You never tried to take Mom's place, but knowing I needed a mother figure, you offered love and guidance. And Dad, you are my hero.

To my sisters: Gwen, throughout my life you have been the "big sister" who could look at things objectively and rationally, the one who still calls me "squirt" even though we're the same height and I'm forty! I'm grateful for all your support. Jackie, thanks for always smiling and making the world seem better than it sometimes is. Thanks for being supportive of everything I do even when no one else "gets it," and for always offering a shoulder and an ear when I need it most. Tina, thanks for being the "strong one" who never gives up and reminds me that I shouldn't, either. I appreciate that you have encouraged me to live out a dream. But most of all, thank you for just being a great sister and someone I know I can always count on.

Jamie: Thanks for your constant love and support, incredible attitude, and belief in me and in "us"; thanks for always knowing when I need comfort, encouragement, or sometimes "a kick in the ass" to push me to my potential. Thanks for loving me and making me happier than I ever thought I could be.

To my wonderful sons, Kyle and Ryan: thanks for being unbelievably patient and understanding with me, especially during this last year. You are more mature than I ever thought about being at your age and much more responsible, too. You have been supportive of my career change into music even though it has been difficult. I hope you know how grateful I am, and how much I love you. You are the best thing I've ever done in my lifetime and I couldn't be more proud.

Philip Lyon: I don't even know where to start thanking you, Philip. You are a big reason I've had so many opportunities in this business, and you have gone above and beyond the call of duty as my attorney. You will forever be a true and wonderful friend. You supported me from day one, with or without a record deal and when I've had no real means of paying for all your services. You also taught me a valuable lesson: "You have two ears and one mouth. When you are meeting someone to talk business, it only makes sense to listen more and talk less." That kept me out of a lot of trouble. Thanks for all of these things and so much more.

Ralph Emery: Thanks for being such a good friend of Mom's all through her career and for letting us use some of your favorite stories in this book. Ralph, Mom so appreciated that time you said she could bring her three little girls into the studio anytime she was booked on your show. You were the best friend a single mom could have.

Del Shores: Thanks for your love of Mom and her music and for believing in me, too. Thanks for the opportunity to work with and become friends with some truly amazing people and for continuing to be such a great friend long after *Sordid Lives* was completed.

Michael Lloyd: Thanks for going to bat for me when I was looking for a record deal. It was such an honor to work with you. You are so incredibly talented yet so easy to work with. I remember attempting to copy Mom's version of "Precious Memories," when you told me to just relax and enjoy myself. I owe you a lot.

Patsi Bale Cox: Thanks so much for all your hard work and the time you put into making this project what we wanted it to be. You are so patient and supportive. I couldn't have done anything without you. Thanks for your insight, your sensitivity, and most important, your friendship. You are a real friend and a great lady. I hope you'll still hang out with this crazy girl after it's all said and done. Thanks for making this part of my dream come true.

The Road Kill Band (my band): Thanks to the best band members I could ever hope for. You were supportive even when our schedule wasn't very busy that first year out. You are like my family, and let's hope we'll be so busy next year, we'll forget how we traveled in a van and U-Haul and took turns driving. Maybe 2011 will bring a bus—or at least an RV.

Thanks to Reggie Mack, Jamie, and Trish Stoner from No Rest Entertainment and to Carrie Moore-Reed for getting me bookings and helping me live out these musical dreams. Without you, I'd just be singing into a hairbrush in my living room.

Special thanks to Mel Berger and William Morris, for believing in this book.

Sarah Durand, our Atria editor: Thanks for your patience and understanding, and for your tremendous talent. You have overseen this "baby" with such compassion. We could not have done it without you. And a thank-you to the rest of the Atria team—Judith Curr, Paul Olsewski, Sarah Cantin, and Jeanne Lee; your vision helped make this the best book it could be.

Special thanks to Val Knust and Marlene Stover for transcriptions.

We often turned to other books during the research for *The Three of Us*. Obviously we relied on the autobiographies Mom and Dad wrote: *Stand By Your Man,* with Joan Dew, and *I Lived to Tell It All,* with Tom Carter. My sister Jackie Daly's book, *A Daughter Recalls,* with Tom Carter, provided many memory prompts. Additional books by Robert K. Oermann and Mary Bufwack, Ralph Emery, Loretta Lynn, and Wynonna Judd helped with time lines and details. And although we may have disagreed with some conclusions, books by Bob Allen and Jimmy McDonough contained helpful details.